The B-24
Liberator
1939-1945

Published in the United States, 1980
by Rand McNally & Company

First published in the United Kingdom
by Wensum Books (Norwich) Ltd.

Copyright © 1979 by Martin Bowman
All rights reserved

Library of Congress Catalog Card Number 80-50342

SBN 528-81538-5

Printed in the United Kingdom

The B-24 Liberator 1939-1945

Martin Bowman

Contents

Introduction 4
Acknowledgements 5
Global Consolidated 6
Man Your Positions 10
The Battle of the Atlantic 12
The Big League 24
Ploesti 36
The Anvil Project 44
Cheek to Cheek, Nose to Tail 52
Pathfinders 56
Assembly 58
Maintenance 60
Death and Destruction 63
Hotel Sweden 66
Black Sheep in Wolves' Clothing 72
Bomber Support Liberators 78
Mediterranean Missions 82
The Forgotten Air Force 96
Over the Hills and Far Away 110
Wings of Gold 112
Pacific Privateers 126
Photo Credits 128

Rand McNally & Company
Chicago • New York • San Francisco

Introduction

This book is not a mission by mission account of every air force to use the Liberator but an overview, recalling in detail aspects of the B-24 which have hitherto received little attention.

This is the first book to detail the activities of the B-24 Liberators of the RAF and US Navy as well as those of the USAAF. Previous publications have paid scant attention to the B-24 in service with the RAF but Liberators carrying the famous blue and red roundels flew many missions over thousands of miles with the South East Asia Command in India and Burma, as well as making a considerable contribution towards combating the U-boats in the Battle of the Atlantic.

The B-24 is perhaps best remembered for its daylight raids with the USAAF 8th and 15th Air Forces and the mission to Ploesti in August 1943, but its greatest impact was in the Pacific with the US Navy where its low-level 'masthead' bombing of Japanese shipping was a constant source of fear to the enemy. The Davis high aspect ratio wing proved ideal for the long, over water patrols at medium altitudes but was never really successful in the European Theatre of Operations where the Liberator was required to fly high altitude bombing missions with the B-17, an aircraft of totally different performance.

The Liberator was produced in far greater numbers than any other American aircraft during the war. It served with fifteen air forces in a wide variety of roles including strategic bombing, maritime reconnaissance, VIP and supply transport, photo-reconnaissance, radio counter measures and as a flying tanker. Its capacious fuselage made it ideal for all these roles, and it proved the most versatile aircraft to serve in the Second World War.

Martin Bowman April 1979, Norwich

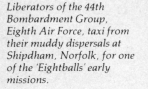

Liberators of the 44th Bombardment Group, Eighth Air Force, taxi from their muddy dispersals at Shipdham, Norfolk, for one of the 'Eightballs' early missions.

Acknowledgments

My pleas for material brought an extraordinary response from both Americans and Britons alike, which far exceeded my expectations and highlights the esteem and affection the Liberator holds for those who flew and serviced her. Many went to great lengths to provide me with photographs and I am extremely grateful to each and every one:

Dennis Allen, Arthur Anderson, Edward Bailey, Wing Commander Geoffrey Bartlett, C. Berry, Bob Bishop, J. J. Berry, H. Bloxham, John Branagan, John Brooks, John F. Burger, Stanley Burgess, R. A. Carty, William L. Case, Len Clarke, Sebastian Corriere, Frank Dalzell, Ron Davies, William Dillon, Fred Dresser, Don Fairbanks, Tony Fairbairn, Deryck Fereday, Peter Fillingham, Bill Foulkes, R. F. Fowler, Ronald French, Peter Frost (Aviation Museum, Flixton), R. F. Gallagher, Stanley M. Gates, James P. Gerrits, R. W. Gwynne, Roland Hammersley, John Hardeman, Tom Henthorne, John Hilderbran, G. Hill, John R. Hirsch, Harry G. Howton, J. S. Hoyle, F. A. Hunt, F. James Arthur Jeffries, Harold Johnston, Archie Jones, J. T. Jones, J. W. Jones, Group-Captain W. J. Jones, Edward T. Keyworth, E. L. Kightley, J. S. Lawrence, L. Loosli, Laurie Lloyd, Dave Mayor, G. Mooney, Frank Mortimer, Edwin Moyle, Douglas Nie, Wiley S. Noble, Torbjorn Olausson, John Page, Bryan Parker, Leslie Parsons, K. O. Phillips, Fred Powers, Don Prutton, George A. Reynolds, Bill Robertie, Max B. Rufner, Dennis R. Scanlon, S. R. Shackleton, A. D. B. Smith, Stefan Soboniewski, Bernard Stevens, Paul F. Stevens, Frank Thomas, Edgar F. Townsend, G. D. Trott, Ernie Wollerston, Bernard Yeomans, Earl Zimmerman. Also Scottish Aviation, General Dynamics, Ford, Douglas and the Imperial War Museum.

Special thanks to Bob McGuire of the B-24 Liberator Club and Mike Bailey, the well known aviation artist, who came to my rescue with some much needed photographic material and technical assistance.

Finally, as always, I must make special mention of my wife Paula whose patience was almost exhausted yet again.

Global Consolidated

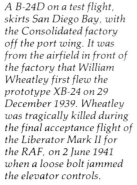

A B-24D on a test flight, skirts San Diego Bay, with the Consolidated factory off the port wing. It was from the airfield in front of the factory that William Wheatley first flew the prototype XB-24 on 29 December 1939. Wheatley was tragically killed during the final acceptance flight of the Liberator Mark II for the RAF, on 2 June 1941 when a loose bolt jammed the elevator controls.

Of all the four-engined bombers built during the Second World War the B-24 Liberator was probably the most versatile. Apart from its bombing role in all theatres of operation, it hauled fuel to France during the push towards Germany, carried troops, fought the U-boat in the Atlantic and, probably most important of all, made a vital contribution towards winning the war in the Pacific. Its most famous single exploit is possibly the raid on the Ploesti oilfields in August 1943. But the B-24 was never to gain the recognition it deserved by press and public alike. Throughout its short operational career the Liberator was overshadowed by its more famous comrade-in-arms, the B-17 Flying Fortress, as was the Halifax by the Lancaster and the Hurricane by the Spitfire. The B-17 'glory boys' looked upon the slab-sided Liberator with disdain, referring to it as 'the crate that ours came in'.

Nevertheless the B-24 Liberator, with its capacious fuselage, which owed much to Consolidated's long pedigree in building flying boats, surpassed the production of every other single type of American military aircraft during the Second World War. Consolidated had a lengthy history in long range aircraft design, led by Isaac Machlin Laddon, who joined the company in 1927 as chief engineer. He was responsible in 1928 for the Admiral flying boat and later the Catalina flying boat, which was to distinguish itself in the Second World War.

In May 1938 the French Government had issued a specification to the Consolidated Aircraft Corporation of San Diego, California, for a heavy bomber. The company's early study, designated LB30, was a landplane version of their new Model 29 flying boat (PB2Y). However, early in 1939 the US Army Air Corps also drew up a requirement for a heavy bomber of infinitely better performance than the Boeing B-17, then in production. They were looking for a bomber capable of a top speed in excess of 300 mph with a range of 3,000 miles and a ceiling of 35,000 feet. Consolidated engineers initiated a further design study designated XB-24, which incorporated David R. Davis's high aspect ratio wing and the twin-finned empennage used on the Model 31 Flying boat (P4Y-1).

By 20 January 1939 preliminary specifications of Model 32—the Liberator—were

ready and construction began. In February a wind tunnel model was tested on the strength of which the designers ventured to Wright Field to discuss their design with senior Air Corps officers. On 30 March 1939 a contract for a prototype was signed after Consolidated had carried out almost thirty changes to the preliminary specifications on the recommendation of the Air Corps.

In September 1939 France followed up its tentative order with a production contract for 139 aircraft under the original LB30 designation. A month later, on 26 October 1939, the Davis wing was first married to the fuselage and on 29 December 1939 the Liberator flew for the first time. William Wheatley was at the controls as it took off from Lindbergh Field next to the Consolidated plant in San Diego.

It could be said that the Liberator was by far the most complicated aircraft yet seen, and certainly the most expensive. The Model 32 was of conventional structure but among the more unusual features was its tricycle undercarriage. The main gears had to be long to exceed the tall bomb bays and were retracted outwards by electric motors. Equally unconventional were the roller-shutter doors protecting the 8,000 lb bomb load which was stowed vertically in the two halves of the bomb bay and separated by a catwalk connecting the flight deck and the tail section.

In 1940 seven YB-24s, which had been ordered by the Air Corps shortly before the contract for the prototype, were delivered for service trials. These aircraft were similar to the prototype but their gross weight had been increased by 5,400 lb to 46,400 lb. The wing leading edge slots had been deleted and de-icing

Above: *The XB-24 prototype.*

Left: *Nose assemblies at the Douglas plant at Tulsa, Oklahoma.*

Below: *The Convair plant at Fort Worth, Texas, assembling B-24Ds with anti-submarine camouflage.*

Bottom: *The Ford plant at Willow Run. Ford produced 6,792 B-24s, and 1,893 in component form.*

boots fitted to the wings and tail. Later that year a further order was placed for thirty-six of the initial B-24 production version. However, only nine aircraft were completed to B-24 standard, which now weighed 53,600 lb and incorporated 0.5 inch machine guns in the tail in place of the 0.30 inch guns of previous models.

One of the original LB-30/ Mark Is delivered to the RAF in August 1941, without turrets and used as transports.

Six YB-24s and twenty B-24As were diverted to the RAF, and after the fall of France in June 1940, Britain took over the French contract for 139 LB30s. As a result of experience gained in combat over Europe the XB-24 was fitted with self-sealing fuel tanks and armour plate.

It is generally believed that the generic name Liberator was selected by the British as it was their custom to give nicknames to aircraft rather than the numerical designations applied by the Americans. However the aircraft was christened Liberator as the result of a contest held at the Consolidated plant in San Diego. Dorothy Fleet, wife of the company's founder, the aviation pioneer Reuben H. Fleet, selected the name and submitted her entry anonymously. It was chosen and adopted despite an attempt in April 1942 by John W. Thompson, Consolidated's public relations officer, to change the name to 'Eagle'.

Meanwhile, in 1941, Consolidated developed the AB-24B, fitted with turbo-supercharged Pratt and Whitney R-1830-41 engines replacing the mechanically supercharged 33s. The substitution was marked with the relocation of the oil coolers on each side of the radial engines instead of underneath and this produced the characteristic elliptical cowling seen on all subsequent models. The aircraft underwent further cosmetic changes with the installation of a Martin dorsal turret and a Consolidated-built tail turret. A further nine more of the 1940 consignment of thirty-six were completed in 1941 as B-24Cs but the first significant version to see service with the USAAF was the B-24D.

The 'D', as it turned out, could well have stood for diverse, the tasks of this aircraft being many and wide ranging. It was basically similar to the B-24C but had uprated engines and the gross weight now stood at 56,000 lb. Contracts were awarded in 1940 and subsequent orders brought the total number of B-24Ds built by 1941 to 2,738, of which 2,425 were constructed by Consolidated-Vultee at San Diego.

During 1942 a second Liberator production line was opened at Fort Worth, Texas, by Convair and this company turned out 303 B-24Ds. A third production line was brought into operation, at Tulsa, where the Douglas Company produced ten B-24Ds before changing production to B-24Es. At the end of 1942 a fourth B-24 production line was opened, by the Ford Motor Company at Willow Run where construction work had begun in 1941. The plant cost 165 million dollars to build and was a quarter of a mile long with seventy assembly lines. It was anticipated that it would employ as many as 100,000 workers once production of the B-24E was in full swing. The first B-24 to be rolled out of its doors was a Consolidated model reassembled at Willow Run from the sub assemblies of two aircraft shipped from San Diego. It was hoped that mass production techniques would speed up the production of Liberators although the rest of the American aviation industry, opposed to Ford's participation in the programme, was cynical. The plant, however, grew from strength to strength.

In early 1943 the fifth and final major manufactory of Liberators was operated by North American at Dallas, Texas. Its first 430 B-24s were designated 'G', the first twenty-five being very similar to the B-24D. The remainder introduced a nose turret containing two 0.50 inch machine guns built by Emerson and Consolidated after experience of head-on attacks in Europe. Variants similar to the 'G' were built by Consolidated at Fort Worth and by Douglas and Ford as the B-24H. Convair built 738 with Emerson nose turrets while Douglas built 582 using Consolidated turrets. Ford surprised the rest of the American aircraft industry with 1,780 B-24Hs containing nose turrets similar to the Consolidated model. And followed up their success with 1,587 B-24Js, which were similar in appearance to the 'H'. All five Liberator manufacturers built this model, which appeared in greater numbers than any other variant. A Motor Products nose turret replaced the Consolidated and Emerson turrets and later incorporated a bomb sight and an auto-pilot. In fact many of the B-24Gs and Hs were redesignated Js when fitted with these two latter devices. Altogether, 6,678 B-24Js were built.

The next model was the B-24L whose main difference was the installation of a Convair-designed tail station which incorporated two hand-held 0.50 inch machine guns. Consolidated built 417 B-24Ls at San Diego while Ford turned out 1,250 at Willow Run. These two factories were the only plants to build the B-24M, of which 916 were manufactured by Convair and 1,677 by Ford.

In August 1941 deliveries to the RAF of the 139 aircraft on the original French contract began and by December that year sixty-five had been delivered to Britain. Many were delivered without turrets and these began operations as transports while the armed version became the Liberator Mark II. The Liberator Mark I was the designation applied to LB30Bs which were modified and armed for use with RAF Coastal Command. The forward bomb bay was sealed off and a gun pack consisting of four 20mm cannon was mounted underneath. The majority of the Mark I 'Sticklebacks' were equipped with early ASV radar antennae on the nose, under the wings and on the top of the rear fuselage. Other LB30Bs flew as transports while LB30As also flew with RAF Transport Command and the Return Ferry Service.

The first Liberators to be used in the bomber role by the RAF were Mark IIs flown by Nos. 159 and 160 Squadrons. All Liberators up to and including the Liberator Mark III (B-24D) were supplied under direct British contracts. The Liberator Mark IIIA and subsequent versions were supplied under Lend-Lease and handed over to the RAF by the USAAF.

A later series B-24D, used in RAF service, was designated the Liberator Mark V, equipped with additional fuel tanks in wing bays and centimetric ASV radar either in a retractable radome in the ventral position aft of the bomb bays or in the 'Dumbo' or 'chin' position. B-24Ds had already been supplied to the Royal Canadian Air Force in September 1943 and twelve others went to the Royal Australian Air Force in 1944. The RCAF Liberators were similar to the RAF Mark II. Deliveries of the 'Dumbo' version were also made to the RCAF.

In November 1943 deliveries of the B Mark VI and GR Mark VI Liberators began. These versions were Convair-built B-24H and J with American turrets except for the tail turret which was by Boulton & Paul. The GR Mark VI anti-submarine aircraft later incorporated a radome containing centimetric radar in place of the ball turret. The B Mark VI was used by RAF squadrons overseas and was also used by the RCAF for training while in the Atlantic and Bay of Biscay. By the end of the war over 1,800 Mark VIs and VIIIs had been used by the RAF, RCAF and RAAF, the greatest number of all models.

In the Middle East the Liberator Mark VI was used mainly against enemy shipping in the Mediterranean. Beginning in July 1944, thirty-six Mark VIIIs were delivered to the RAF in that theatre, each equipped with centimetric radar designed for PFF operations against ground targets. In the Far East the Liberator Mark VI was the principal bomber used in the final Burma campaign ending with the capture of Rangoon. Fresh deliveries of Mark VIIIs arrived in May 1945.

By the end of the war almost 2,500 Liberators of one sort or another had been delivered to the RAF, RCAF and the RAAF of which 1,694 were supplied by Consolidated alone.

In 1943 a B-24D was modified into the XB-24K by Ford's at Willow Run by the addition of

Above: *The XB-24N, single-finned Liberator on an early test flight.*

Left: *Winston Churchill poses in the cockpit of his VIP transport* Commando *during his visit to Turkey in April 1943. A crescent and star were specially painted for the occasion. The hammer and sickle denote a previous vist to Russia. This LB-30 was replaced by an RY-3 single-finned transport version of the US Navy PB4Y 'Privateer' in 1944.*

a single fin and rudder. General stability and control were always inferior to the B-17 but it was discovered that the single-finned machine produced greater stability and improved performance. Armament was also revised and a ball turret was fitted to the nose. Ford built seven YB-24Ns to begin production but 5,168 B-24Ns on order at Willow Run were cancelled on 31 May 1945 when the war in Europe ended. Perhaps the most famous single-finned Liberator was a Mark II used by Winston Churchill as his own personal transport known as *Commando*.

Below: *B-24Ls at the Ford plant at Willow Run are parked pending delivery to a modification centre for installation of hand held guns.*

Man Your Positions

Above: *A B-24L showing the Emerson turret, cockpit, and navigator's window. The latter was enlarged as the nose turret obscured visibility.*

Above Right: *An RAF Bomb-aimer (Bombardier) in the nose of a B-24D.*

Below Right: *A tunnel gunner posing with a 0.50 machine gun. Prior to installation of ball turrets.*

Below: *Waist gunners aboard a Pacific based Liberator wearing flak vests.*

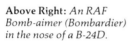

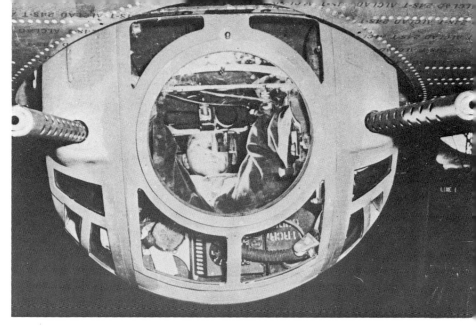

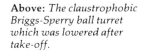

Above: *The claustrophobic Briggs-Sperry ball turret which was lowered after take-off.*

Left Top: *An unknown pilot at the controls of PB4Y-1 Liberator at Dunkeswell.*

Left Centre: *A Martin electrically driven mid-upper turret on a Mark BVI in India. The Hatch to the left is for dinghy stowage.*

Left Bottom: *An RAF Tail Gunner prepares his Browning 0.50 machine guns. Air gunners ideally could not be more than five feet ten inches tall, or weigh more than 160 pounds.*

Right Top: *Before tail turrets, 0.50 Brownings were hand held on flexible mountings. This is a field modification made in North Africa.*

Right Centre: *Cleaning the muzzle of a 0.50 Browning in the Convair tail turret.*

Right Bottom: *A Boulton & Paul tail turret with .303 Brownings.*

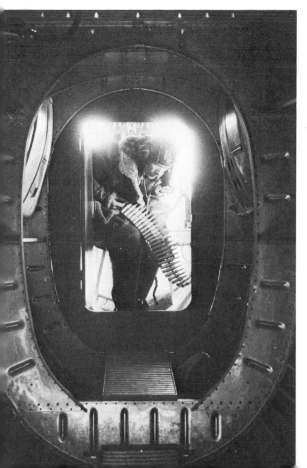

The Battle of the Atlantic

The Battle of the Atlantic was very nearly lost in the dark winter of 1942-43 and the frightful spring which followed it. British naval historians considered that the war was almost lost for the lack of two squadrons of very long range aircraft; twenty-four Lancasters would have filled the bill.

N. W. Emmott in
Proceedings of the US Naval Institute
May 1969.

Until the spring of 1940 the war at sea had gone steadily in Britain's favour. Even the Germans' victorious campaign had cost the Kriegsmarine one-third of its cruisers and almost half its destroyers. However, Germany's occupation of Norway and the subsequent overrunning of France and the Low Countries and Italy's intervention in the war changed the situation radically. U-boats and E-boats began operating with deadly effect from French Atlantic bases. Soon aircraft such as the four-engined Focke-Wulf 200, an adapted commercial transport with a range of 2,000 miles, began to menace Britain's Western Approaches and reach out into mid-Atlantic waters previously immune from German intervention.

RAF Coastal Command was at once confronted with a series of fresh problems ranging from anti-invasion patrols to long-range escort duties. In June 1940 Air Chief Marshal Sir Frederick Bowhill could only call upon 500 aircraft for such diverse tasks and only thirty-four of these, the Sunderlands, could operate beyond 500 miles from Britain's shores. At first the U-boats attacked shipping in the South West Approaches but by August they became bolder, following up on the surface during the day and delaying closing in on convoys until nightfall. To escape detection by the Asdics they remained on the surface and attacked under cover of darkness. Coastal Command did not have an answer to such tactics and from the beginning of June to the end of 1940 over 300 million tons of Allied and neutral merchant shipping was sunk.

By the middle of 1941 the shortage of very long range aircraft, as opposed to long-range aircraft was still causing problems. As the U-boat campaign intensified stop gap measures were tried, such as procuring Blenheims from Bomber Command. Bases were established

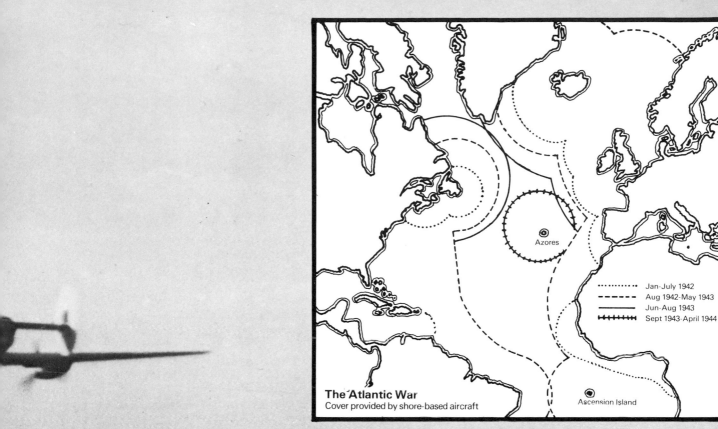

The Atlantic War
Cover provided by shore-based aircraft

Azores

Ascension Island

············ Jan-July 1942
– – – – – Aug 1942-May 1943
———— Jun-Aug 1943
+++++++ Sept 1943-April 1944

in the Hebrides, Northern Ireland and Iceland but very valuable locations were denied the British in Eire. By May 1941 the U-boats were largely reduced to operating off West Africa or in the Central Atlantic, the latter being beyond the range of Coastal Command aircraft.

In June 1941 Bowhill was posted to form Ferry Command while Air Marshal Sir Philip Joubert took over Coastal Command. Joubert inherited a force of forty squadrons and more than half the aircraft were now fitted with ASV (Air to Surface Vessel) radar. Joubert's overriding task was to increase the effectiveness of his ASV aircraft and create airborne U-boat killers. He pressed for heavier types of anti-submarine bombs, bomb sights for low level attack, and depth charge pistols which would detonate at less than fifty feet below the surface. He encouraged tests, first started by Bowhill, with various forms of camouflage, in order to render the attacker invisible for as long as possible. As a result all anti U-boat aircraft were painted white on their sides and undersurfaces.

By September 1941 the increased shipping losses again prompted the Admiralty to explore the possibility of employing bombers in the war at sea. Bomber Command had steadfastly refused to allocate any four-engined bombers to Coastal Command but had turned over large numbers of two-engined Whitleys, Wellingtons and Blenheims. Ironically there was a four-engined bomber available to the hard-pressed Coastal Command—the Liberator. But Coastal Command could only muster one Liberator squadron, No. 120, which was then based at Nutts Corner, Northern Ireland. The Liberator was capable of very long range and therefore ideal for forays in the mid-Atlantic.

The shipping losses in October and November showed a reduction over those of September, although the autumn gales and the redeployment of the U-boat packs to the Mediterranean were partly responsible. Hitler, worried by Britain's successful offensive on Axis convoys *en route* for Libya, sent packs of U-boats to the Mediterranean and although several were sunk, eighteen got through. In November HMS *Ark Royal* and HMS *Barham* were sunk and additional air cover was

A Liberator Mark IIIA practices periscope bombing at the Thorney Island range in Pagham Harbour, probably October 1942.

LIBERATOR I
TWIN WASP-S3C

A Liberator Mark I 'stickleback' pictured in July 1941 and showing the early ASV radar and 20mm cannon pack under the fuselage. During ground testing the bomb bay doors were known to cave in although this was not repeated in flight.

immediately sent to Gibraltar.

On 14 December 1941 Convoy HG76 sailed under escort from Gibraltar. By the morning of 17 December the convoy was out of air range of the Rock and over the next four days nine U-boats preyed on the convoy, sinking two merchant vessels, a destroyer and the auxiliary carrier HMS *Audacity*. However four U-boats were sunk and two Condors brought down. The thinned ranks of HG76 carried on until at 10.54 hours on the 22 December when it was met 750 miles out from Nutts Corner by a Liberator of 120 Squadron. This aircraft immediately went into action, driving off a Condor shadowing the convoy and then, two hours later, sighting and attacking a U-boat. At 16.20 hours another Liberator took over and within three hours had forced three more U-boats to submerge. By the time fuel shortage forced the Liberator to turn for home the U-boats had been sufficiently discouraged and the convoy was molested no further.

In January 1942 six of Germany's largest U-boats arrived in North American waters to counter the USA's involvement in the war. Within three weeks forty Allied ships, totalling 23,000 tons, were sunk. American defences had still not been tightened up when Doenitz ordered all his U-boats west of the British Isles, and several more lying off the Azores, to take up station on the North American and Central American seaboards. America responded by involving Liberators of the 44th and 93rd Bomb Groups, which were earmarked for the Eighth Air Force in England, in anti-submarine patrols. Ted Timberlake's 93rd, based at Fort Myers, Florida, was involved in anti-submarine duties over the Gulf of Mexico and along the coast of Cuba for three months beginning in May 1942. The 44th Bomb Group at Barkesdale Field also took part in U-boat operations in the Gulf and was credited with the sinking of one enemy submarine. In all, three U-boat kills were credited to the 93rd Bomb Group. But by the end of May 1942 the U-boat packs had wrought havoc, sinking 109 ships in that month alone. However there was one consolation. With the U-boats otherwise engaged, the majority of convoys plying between North America and Britain escaped virtually unscathed for a few months. In waters protected by Coastal Command only nine merchant vessels were sunk in five months.

In June 1942 there was a vast improvement in U-boat kills in the Bay of Biscay. Coastal Command had been helped by the transfer of a squadron of Whitleys and eight Liberators from Bomber Command in April and other aircraft were to follow. Advances, too, were made in the technical field. New depth charges, filled with Torpex (which was 30 per cent more effective than Amatol) were introduced. The fitting of the Mark XIIIQ pistol ensured detonation at thirty-four feet below the surface, although this was deeper than the ideal of twenty-five feet.

Very early in the war Coastal Command had realized that their anti-submarine aircraft would need something more reliable than the quickly consumed flares they were using at night to illuminate U-boats. As a result in 1940 Squadron Leader H. de B. Leigh was encouraged by the then Chief of Coastal Command, Air Chief Marshal Bowhill, to develop the idea of an airborne searchlight. Leigh experimented with a twenty-four inch searchlight in the under-turret of a mine-detonating Wellington and eventually by substituting batteries for the generator the Leigh Light won acceptance over the heavier Helmore Turbinlite developed originally for night fighting.

The Leigh Light operator had to switch on the light at the last possible moment just as the ASV reading was disappearing from the radar screen because the blip, which grows clearer up to about three quarters of a mile from the target, then becomes merged in the general returns from the sea's surface. The detected object was trapped and held in the beam allowing the crew to release its bombs.

Despite early misgivings at the Air Ministry a full squadron of Leigh Light Wellingtons was formed in February 1942 and by June they had proved so successful that Doenitz ordered all U-boats to proceed submerged at all times except when it was necessary to re-charge batteries. The morale of U-boat crews slumped with the knowledge that darkness no longer afforded them protection. During July 1942 the Leigh Light Wellingtons chalked up their first U-boat kill and the following month the Air Ministry approved the formation of a second squadron. At the same time nacelle type Leigh Lights were ordered for all Catalinas and trial installations approved for the Liberators and Fortresses.

But the Germans were determined to counter continued Allied organisation and ingenuity and Doenitz managed to persuade Goering to let him have 24 Junkers JU-88s for operations in the Bay of Biscay. He was further helped by the sudden appearance of large fleets of French fishing vessels which began operating at night. The blip produced on the ASV screen by a tunnyman was indistinguishable from that of a U-boat. Each time Leigh Light operators exposed their searchlights to light up a fishing vessel they compromised their own position and were needlessly running down their batteries. By mid-August 1942 the French fishing fleet was so widespread that night operations against U-boats virtually came to a halt. Despite appeals, leaflet dropping and threats of capture or shooting up the vessels, only the end of the season brought relief.

A more serious problem was caused by the knowledge that the Germans had obtained an ASV Mark II set from a Hudson which had unfortunately crashed in Tunisia. By mid-September 1942 the Germans had developed the Metox 600, capable of receiving and recording ASV transmission from up to thirty miles, and had fitted it to large numbers of their U-boats. This enabled them to dive well before they were sighted by anti-submarine aircraft. An attempt to flood the Bay of Biscay with ASV transmission failed and by January 1943 Coastal Command aircraft had almost ceased to locate U-boats by night. The only answer was to replace the ASV Mark II, which only had a one and half metre wavelength, with the long overdue ASV Mark III of ten centimetres wavelength. This apparatus was already in operation having originated from an adaptation of centimetric AI. An American version, developed with the help of British scientists, had been tested successfully in May 1942. Within a few months USAAF Liberators on anti-submarine duties in the Western Hemisphere had been equipped with these or similar sets but by August 1942 it was evident that first British models would not be available until spring 1943.

Meanwhile, with U-boat packs prevented from finding any rich pickings in waters five hundred miles from Anglo-American air bases, Doenitz was forced to concentrate his forces in the 'Greenland Gap' and the 'Azores Gap' where Allied air patrols could not penetrate. The only solution was to close the gaps using carrier-borne or very long range land based aircraft. In August 1942 there were no aircraft carriers or auxiliary carriers available for trans-Atlantic convoys while there were only five VLR Liberator Is (from 120 Squadron) in the whole of Coastal Command. These aircraft had an operational range of 2,400 miles while the Squadron's remaining Liberator Mark IIs and IIIs could only extend 1,800 miles and 1,680 miles respectively. Air Vice Marshal John C. Slessor undertook a special mission to Washington to speed up the supply of Liberators.

Two Hudson squadrons, Nos. 59 and 224, began converting to the Liberator but neither was operational until October 1942. Flight Lieutenant John Brooks, a flight engineer on Liberators, recalls converting 224 Squadron from two-engined Hudsons to the Liberator.

'Sixteen Liberator IIs and Vs were flown in between October and December 1942 from the USA to the Scottish Aviation works at Prestwick. All the necessary modifications to convert the high altitude bombers to anti-submarine aircraft were carried out. Defensive armament was largely stripped out and radar and British navigation equipment installed. (The stripping out of defensive armament was later abandoned as the enemy stepped up its fighter patrols in the Bay of Biscay in the defence of its U-boat force.) Crew training went remarkably smoothly but was hampered to some extent by the poor weather of the Western Isles and the unsuitability of the runways which were merely strips of tarmac laid on to the sandy soil of Tiree.

'The weight of the Liberators soon created a wave pattern at the touchdown points at the end of the runway and were temporarily filled in with wooden chips. The months of August and September were spent in type training exercises, circuits and landings, navigational and wireless exercises and air gunnery practice. On 25 August crews were formed and operational exercises carried out in co-operation with Royal Navy submarines and fighter aircraft. At the end of August the squadron moved to Beaulieu in the New Forest in Hampshire and became operational, flying convoy escorts and anti-submarine sweeps in the Bay of Biscay in October.'

In the meantime 120 Squadron continued to bear the brunt of anti-submarine duties in the Atlantic. Edward Bailey, a WOM/AIR, joined the pioneer RAF Liberator squadron in September 1942 at Nutts Corner. The Northern Ireland base was not without its problems as he recalls:

'The main Belfast to Londonderry railway line crossed one runway and railway signals were operated from flying control before we could take off. I was appointed to a crew undergoing squadron training and spent a few months on ground and air training prior to becoming operational. Practice navigational flights were made to various positions over the Atlantic and sometimes we had to locate

Liberator ZZ-K of 220 Squadron showing the Leigh Light under the starboard wing.

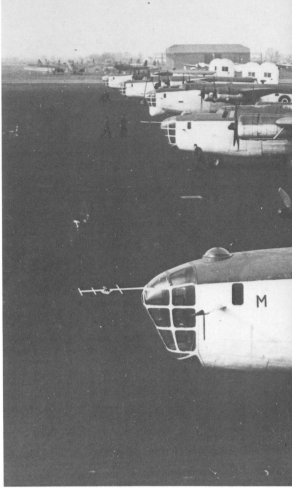

Top: *A GRV Liberator stands at dispersal at Balllykelly, Northern Ireland. During operations traffic lights were operated for the railway line which bisected the runway.*

Centre: *A Liberator Mark IIIA of 59 Squadron.*

Bottom: *A 224 Squadron 'Dumbo' Liberator being modified at the Scottish Aviation Works at Prestwick in 1942.*

Rockall. There was also gunnery and bombing practice over Loch Neagh with 10 lb smoke bombs. The flight engineer loaded these bombs while we were in flight and it was considered 'infra dig' for the pilot to open the bomb doors while the engineer was carrying out this task!

'We had about two Liberator Mark Is and the rest were Mark IIIs. The Mark I had no rear turret but had a 0.5 machine gun mounted in the tail protected by curved doors which could slide open for firing. Under the fuselage, just forward of the bomb bay, were mounted four cannon which we used when going into attack on the U-boats. Inside the aircraft we had a rudimentary cooking stove and a sleeping bunk just rear of the bomb bay which was very useful on the long seagoing patrols. At the time of my arrival the Liberator Mark Is were just going

out of service and most operations were carried out by the Mark IIIs.'

Steps had been taken to help shorten the gap between American air patrols from Newfoundland and Nova Scotia and British air patrols from Iceland and Northern Ireland. In August 1942 Britain had asked the Royal Canadian Air Force if they could extend their anti-submarine and convoy protection sorties to 800 miles to help close part of the Atlantic gap but this was not possible as the first Canadian Liberators did not arrive until April 1943.

In September 1942, 120 Squadron provided a detachment of Liberators in Iceland. The strategic value of this remote island in the North Atlantic had been recognized as far back as 1940 when British forces forestalled a German invasion and landed at Reykjavik. Liberators from 120 Squadron operated from an airfield on the south east edge of the capital. Edward Bailey recalls the procedure for a typical operation:

'The crew were called (often in the early hours) three hours before take-off and pilots, navigator and the 1st WOP or WOM went to the operations room for briefing. We then had a 'flying meal' (very good considering it was wartime) before loading the Liberator with parachutes, individual dinghies, Mae Wests and flying rations. In winter we sometimes had to help sweep snow off the main plane before we could take off. We always took off from Iceland using maximum boost. The runway

was rather short and take-off with a full load and a cross wind could be difficult. Towards the end of 1943 we flew unladen to another airfield with a longer runway where we loaded up and took off.

'After becoming airborne, the crew who stayed on the flight deck for take-off got into their positions. The navigator went to his place in the nose. When the pilot had set course and adjusted the trim of the aircraft, one WOP/AG went to the rear turret and another went either to the radar or the nose to keep a lookout and the third took up a listening watch on the radio, ready to transmit messages if necessary. These three changed their positions every hour. Every half hour the weather report from Reykjavik was received.

'After about four hours of flying, fuel from the overload tanks in the bomb bay was transferred to the main wing tanks. On escort duties with convoys it was the Senior Naval Officer (SNO) who instructed the captain of the aircraft where he wished the search (often a square search) made. The length of time the Liberator stayed on patrol was generally left to the captain of the aircraft but normally it was about six to seven hours.

'As weather conditions in Iceland were extremely variable weather reports were vital. If the weather closed in over Iceland, the aircraft had to be diverted to Northern Ireland or the Hebrides. On this tour all navigation was carried out by dead reckoning which demanded great skill and hard work from the navigator—

ours was very good. The navigator was the one member of the crew who had to work flat out for the whole length of the trip. Pilots could put the Liberator on 'George', the automatic pilot and although vigilance was essential from all members of the crew, a certain amount of relaxation was permitted. The navigator however had no chance to relax.'

Shipping losses in the Atlantic continued to

Top: Liberator Mark IIIs and IVs of 120 Squadron at Aldergrove, Northern Ireland in April 1943.

Below: *A Coastal Command GRV Liberator on its final approach to Iceland after a long Atlantic patrol.*

Top: *A US Navy PB4Y-1 Liberator of Squadron VB-110 patrolling the Bay of Biscay in late 1943.*

Below: *Ground staff toil on Liberators basking in the sun at III0TU, Windsor Field, Nassau in the Bahamas. The Liberators of Transport Command operated a scheduled ferry service between Florida, the Bahamas, and the Gold Coast—a distance of 3000 miles.*

A beam-gunner (waist-gunner in USAAF) on an RAF Coastal Command Liberator armed with a Colt Browning M-2 0.50 calibre machine-gun. Note the flak eliminator on the muzzle and the wind deflector forward of the waist hatch in the open position.

mount and in October 1942 temporary relief was provided by the 330th and 409th Bomb Squadrons of the 93rd Bomb Group belonging to the Eighth Air Force. This Group had previously experienced anti-submarine duties in the Gulf of Mexico. On 25 October 1942 the 330th Squadron was transferred from its base at Alconbury to Holmsley South, Hampshire, while the 409th began operations from St Eval in Cornwall. That month No. 86 (RAF) Squadron began receiving Liberators and acting as a training unit for No. 160 Squadron until February 1943, when it received its own Liberators and in March began moving to Northern Ireland where it also flew anti-submarine patrols. 160 Squadron had already begun converting from Hudsons in August 1942 at Thorney Island with Liberators from 59 Squadron. By 24 October 1942 four crews were deemed fully operational and made eleven to twelve hour anti-submarine escorts for a convoy well out in the North Atlantic, landing back at St Eval, Cornwall. From then the number of sorties by day and night built up rapidly and various actions took place in the Bay of Biscay and the Channel approaches, including at least three genuine U-boat attacks without radar, which was not then fitted.

Towards the end of 1942 Coastal Command was forced once more to diversify its operational strategy. The invasion of French North Africa placed considerable strain on the already overworked command which carried out photo-reconnaissance missions over French and Italian naval bases as well as the area where 'Operation Torch' would land. In addition, meteorological flights were flown far out over the Atlantic and a constant vigil maintained over German capital ships lurking in Norwegian fjords. Most important of all, the number of anti-submarine patrols in the Bay of Biscay and the waters around Gibraltar had to be stepped up to protect the convoys heading for North Africa.

Coastal Command airfields in the West Country were developed to meet the increase in operations. St Eval was converted to take seventy-two aircraft while Chivenor was organised for a peak compliment of eighty-eight aircraft. Coastal Command aircraft and the Liberators of the 93rd's 330th and 409th Squadrons, on detached duty with the RAF, were fully committed to 'Torch' operation, providing long range protection duties for the invasion fleet scouring the Bay of Biscay for up to twelve hours at a time searching for the elusive U-boats. Despite a handful of sightings, no attacks were made.

At the last minute the Royal Navy asked for more air support for the additional convoys. Joubert was permitted to borrow a Canadian Halifax squadron from Bomber Command and eight Liberators from the Eighth Air Force in East Anglia. These provided excellent cover and the only two U-boats which were seen to approach their line of passage were sunk by two Liberators belonging to 224 Squadron. They undoubtedly saved the operation from further trouble and on 2 November the first convoys came within reach of air cover provided from Gibraltar. German aircraft put in an appearance in November and two attacks were met by Liberators of the 93rd Bomb Group detachment. The most memorable clash occured on 21 November when Major Ramsey D. Potts of the 330th was faced with an ouslaught of five Junkers Ju-88s. Undaunted the B-24 gunners, aided by the Germans' cumbersome approach, dispatched two and damaged a third. In late November both squadrons, having provided excellent service over the Bay of Biscay, returned to Alconbury.

The training of RAF Liberator crews posed something of a problem. An environment free of interruption from enemy aircraft was needed and by the end of 1942 two large construction programmes by the Americans enabled RAF 111 Operational Training Unit to start flying on the island of New Providence in the Bahamas. Oakes Field, the principal base, had a main East-West runway of 6,000 feet carved out of coral rocks and was used for operational training with a fleet of about forty B-25 Mitchell light bombers. Having successfully passed out of this phase of training, the aircrews moved to the other end of the island to the satellite station of Windsor Field which had 7,000 foot runways occupied by nearly thirty Liberators. Here the syllabus culminated in a very long flight over the sea almost to Bermuda and back searching for a small group of RN ships on anti-submarine exercises. Finally, the crews went to Canada and their ultimate destinations in UK or ACSEA Liberator squadrons. Besides RAF, the training intakes included batches of Czech, Canadian, Australian and New Zealand air force personnel. They came by way of the Canadian training organization and were joined by others who had already completed a tour of operations on other aircraft (mainly Hudsons) in the UK.

Air crews started coming through to Coastal Command with regularity but aircraft like the badly needed Liberators were still in short supply. In late March 1943, 59 Squadron returned to Thorney Island to re-equip with Liberators for the second time. Now it was the much-modified VLR (Very Long Range) Liberator V, stripped of much of its armour and armament but able to lift 2000 gallons of fuel and still carry eight 250 lb depth charges. That month the 1st and 2nd Anti-submarine Squadrons moved to Port Lyautey in North Africa and in June became units of the 480th Anti-submarine Group. During June 1943, the 4th and 6th Anti-submarine Squadrons arrived at St Eval to form the 479th Anti-submarine Group and begin operations in the Bay of Biscay, known to American crews as 'Outer Gondola'. In August 1943 they moved to Dunkeswell, Devon where they were joined by the 19th and 22nd ASSs. In September-October 1943 the 478th was dispersed and their duties were taken over by three US Navy Squadrons from Fleet Air Wing Seven—VB 103, VB 105 and VB 110. (VPB after October 1944). Apart from these squadrons Fleet Admiral Ernest King, USN, showed a tendency to keep powerful anti-submarine forces in areas close to

the Americans' own Atlantic seaboard and in the approaches to the Mediterranean where they could protect their own convoys.

Valuable anti-submarine aircraft had been lost during 'Operation Torch' when control of RAF Gibraltar was temporarily transferred from Coastal Command to the Air Officer Commanding in French North Africa. It was not until 8 October 1943, when an air base was established in the Azores as the result of an agreement between Great Britain and Portugal, that the Gibraltar squadrons were returned. In 1944 a somewhat curious US Navy PB4Y-1 marking occurred due to diplomatic reasons when US Navy PB4Y-1s based in the Azores were forced to display RAF roundels as well as the American star and bar insignia.

Edward Bailey's crew with 120 Squadron in Iceland had become operational in January 1943 and had commenced anti-U-boat patrols

Top: *A PB4Y-1 in flight over Colebrook, Devon during a patrol over the Bay of Biscay.*

Below: *A PB4Y-1 based in the Azores displays dual Allied markings to conform with Portugese neutrality.*

Bottom: *Liberators of 220 Squadron in the Azores, 18 April 1945.*

over the North Atlantic: 'The longest trip we made was sixteen and a half hours although some crews flew trips of eighteen hours duration. On 5 April 1943, when escorting convoy HX231, we sighted and attacked our first U-boat. It was sighted by the captain from his 1st pilots position. The normal flying height while on patrol was about 1,000 feet depending on the height of the cloud base and attacks were generally made at about fifty feet. Though evasive action was taken during the run in, it was important that just before the release of the depth charges, flight was straight and level. On this occasion we dropped a stick of four depth charges close to the U-boat and the result was a probable kill. An automatic camera, located under the rear portion of the fuselage, and a hand-held camera, operated by the rear gunner, were used to provide evidence. Before and during the attacks the WOP transmitted a sighting report and an attack report to base and held down the morse key so that ground stations could take a fix on the plane's position.

'On 14 May 1943 we attacked another U-boat while on convoy escort and five days later we attacked two more U-boats. This latter operation lasted fifteen hours. As the U-boats stayed on the surface and fired a 3.7mm gun from this position in the stern of the conning tower, there was always a strong possibility of being shot down. In 1943 a 0.5 inch machine gun was mounted in the perspex nose compartment of the Liberator to upset the U-boat gun crews. We were lucky but at least two Liberators were believed to have been brought down while making such attacks. The chances of surviving in a dinghy (assuming one made a successful ditching) in the North Atlantic were considered very slim.'

In May 1943, 53 Squadron replaced its ageing Whitleys with Liberators and for the following sixteen months flew patrols from Northern Ireland over the Channel and the Bay of Biscay before moving to Iceland in September 1944. During May 1943 they were joined in Northern Ireland at Aldergrove by 59 Squadron. Their Liberators carried the ten top secret Mark 24 American acoustic torpedoes which revolutionized the task of killing U-boats. The Mark 24 was popularly known as 'FIDO' or 'Wandering Annie' although it was a criminal offence even to discuss it. It entered service in May 1943 and was found to be a most effective weapon against U-boats which had just dived. A Liberator from 86 Squadron and a US Navy Catalina belonging to VP-84 each sank a U-boat with the device on 14 May 1943.

During June 1943 224 Squadron Liberators were also given more 'teeth'. Extra waist guns and gunners were carried during the squadron's anti U-boat sweeps in the Bay of Biscay. The squadron was now based at St. Eval and one of its advantages was that the officers were billeted at the Watergate Bay Hotel and the NCOs at two hotels at Porth Bay near Newquay, Cornwall. From June onwards 224 Squadron hunted the U-boat packs in the Bay supplemented by ever-increasing numbers of Liberators from 59 Squadron and others. John Branagan, a Liberator WOP-air gunner on his second tour of operations, recalls a memorable operation with 59 Squadron at Aldergrove:

'On 29 July we took off at 03.50 hours for a special escort for a large convoy heading for Britain. When we arrived one ship was on fire and ships were being attacked by a Focke-Wulf 200 using high level bombing technique. The Senior Naval Officer of the convoy instructed us by radio to attack the enemy aircraft, which now numbered seven! To climb we had to lose weight. We dared not jettison our lethal cargo or we would have sunk almost half the convoy so we flew on about thirty miles and jettisoned our bomb load in the sea. We then broadcast a coded signal to our headquarters and headed back to the convoy.

'We got on the tail of a Focke-Wulf which was going into attack but the gunners on the ships let all hell loose. They fired at the Focke-Wulf 200 and ourselves but caused the enemy aircraft to swerve just as he was dropping his bombs. His missed his target altogether and to our amazement all seven Condors broke off the action and scurried for home. They may have intercepted our radio message calling for reinforcements on the emergency air attack code. It was probably just as well for them because at first light the following day eight Liberators from 59 Squadron arrived to protect the convoy. Our total flying time on this mission was fifteen hours thirty five minutes.'

U-boat operations were not always centred on the Bay of Biscay and mid-Atlantic. Not so well known are the anti U-boat operations

Consolidated PB4Y-1s of US Navy Squadron VB-110 at Dunkeswell, Devon in early 1944.

carried out from North West Africa. In August 1943 No. 22 Squadron, based at Bathurst in the Gambia, began exchanging its Hudsons for Liberators. On 11 August Liberator *D for Dog*, piloted by Flying Officer L. A. Trigg of the RNAF, was on anti-submarine patrol off the coast of West Africa. Trigg sighted U.468 about 240 miles south west of Dakar and went into the attack. The U-boat was on the surface and prepared to defend herself with anti-aircraft guns. The Liberator was hit repeatedly and was on fire in several places when it arrived in a position to attack. Undaunted, the depth charges were released and within twenty minutes U.468 was sinking beneath the waves. However, the stricken *D for Dog* perished with her, a victim of the submarine's anti-aircraft fire. Trigg and his gallant crew died but one of the Liberator's dinghies, released by the impact, floated clear and enabled some of the U-boat's crew to climb to safety. Their evidence was subsquently taken into account and Trigg was posthumously awarded the Victoria Cross, Britain's highest military decoration.

In September 1943, 120 Squadron ceased flying anti-submarine patrols between their base in Iceland, the Westmanear Islands and The Faeroes and reverted to convoy protection patrols in the North Atlantic just south of Cape Farewell. On 30 September 1943 they were joined by a detachment of 59 Squadron Liberators. John Branagan recalls:

'We landed at Reykjavik but the runway was too short for the Liberator Mark VIII. We almost hit a hospital at the end of the runway. After that experience we were transferred to Meeks Field, Keflavik, and became the first RAF aircraft to operate there. It was rather primitive but the Americans were very friendly and sociable, no doubt encouraged by our supplies of whisky and spirits. The American authorities had decreed that because Iceland was a 'dry' country at that time, all Americans stationed there should be 'dry' also!

'On 17 October 1943 we sighted a U-boat and destroyed it. It was one of a large concentration reported in the vicinity of a big Atlantic convoy somewhere south of Greenland. Having heard that U-boats were fighting it out on the surface and that one Liberator had been shot down we remained very alert. Towards the end of our patrol we spotted a U-boat on the surface

travelling at about eight knots. It immediately opened fire with everything it had. I was just changing over from the radar to the radio and the bomb doors were open when I saw tracer shells passing under the wings. We dived down to attack. I ordered our young flight engineer, who was standing on the flight deck wondering what to do, to man the 0.5 inch beam gun and be careful not to shoot our tail off because there was no restrictor gear. Then I resumed my position on the radio ready to broadcast if

Above: A U-boat falls victim to a Coastal Command Liberator in the Atlantic.

A GRV Liberator of Coastal Command showing rocket rails.

necessary. The second pilot handed me a message in code which read "I am attacking enemy submarine on surface", and went on to state the time and our position. My morse was not exactly perfect because of the noise of the guns and the swerving of the aircraft. Reception from our Iceland base was bad and I failed to contact them. Here is where professional operators at other headquarters showed their merit. First of all 15 Group at Liverpool acknowledged, closely followed by St Johns, Newfoundland and, strange as it might seem, Gibraltar! I finally managed to contact Iceland via Liverpool.

Once more we circled the U-boat and dropped our second salvo of charges. The German crew scrambled out through the conning tower and abandoned ship. Seconds later it exploded and broke in half, leaving about thirty survivors in the sea. I broadcast again to Iceland to signal the result of our engagement with the enemy. We landed back at Keflavik after being in the air for sixteen hours forty five minutes.'

In October 1943 some Liberators became very formidable indeed. They were fitted with rockets to carry out attacks on U-boats which stayed on the surface to fight it out. Some B-24s were also fitted with long range tanks in the forward bomb bays giving a total endurance of nineteen hours. Some Mark Vs were also equiped with eight million candle power Leigh Lights mounted under the outer starboard wing and others fitted with sona buoys and modified to carry ninety anti-tank bombs converted for use against U-boats.

Other aircraft were trying to make it as difficult as possible for German ships to make use of the seas within range of Great Britain. To operate the blockade, surface vessels and submarines of the Royal Navy were helped by

anti-submarine aircraft of No. 19 Group operating from Plymouth. One of the squadrons allotted the task of intercepting blockade runners was 311 (Czechoslovak) Squadron based at Aldergrove, Northern Ireland. During the summer of 1943 this unit had converted from Wellingtons to Liberators and in December distinguished itself with a particularly gallant attack.

On the morning of 27 December 1943 the German vessel *Alsterufer* was spotted by a Sunderland heading from the South Atlantic for Bordeaux. Canadian Sunderlands were sent to bomb the 2,729 ton ship but failed to sink her. The Luftwaffe and the Kriegsmarine failed to bring relief and at 16.07 hours *H for How* from 311 Squadron made its attack. The Liberator roared in at low level raking the ship with all its machine guns despite fierce anti-aircraft fire and small mines fired into the air which descended on parachutes. The Czech crew fired rockets and then bombed the *Alsterufer* with 250 lb bombs from only 600 feet. Five of the rockets found their mark and both bombs opened up the hold, killing two ratings on the mess deck inexplicably playing chess at the time to soothe their shattered nerves. The *Alsterufer* began to burn fiercely and the crew abandoned ship. However the vessel did not sink for four hours and her demise was hastened by two Liberators of 86 Squadron. Seventy-four survivors were later rescued and many paid grudging respect to the Czech Liberator crew which they said had flown 'unperturbed through the heaviest barrage'. No. 311 Squadron operated Leigh Light Liberators during the closing months of the war and in June 1945 transferred to Trooping Command.

Meanwhile during the closing months of 1943, 120 Squadron was heavily involved in several U-boat engagements. Edward Bailey's crew attacked them on six occasions during convoy escort duties. In January 1944, 120 Squadron continued anti-submarine sweeps operating from Iceland. The following month Bailey and his fellow crew members completed their tour of operations and went on 'rest' leave as instructors at training units. In March 1944, 120 Squadron was replaced in Iceland by 86 Squadron and returned to Northern Ireland, flying patrols from there until the end of the war. Edward Bailey joined 86 Squadron in February 1945 to begin his second tour of operations:

'This squadron was now equipped with the Liberator Mark VI and VIII. The Boulton & Paul turret had been replaced by American turrets in the nose and tail and each contained two 0.5 machine guns. The wireless operator's position was now over the bomb bay and the radar operator's on the flight deck. Single 0.5 machine guns were mounted in each of the beam positions although great care still had to be taken not to shoot one's tail off because there was still no interrupter gear. There was now two navigators in the crew and the aircraft was fitted with various electronic navigational aids.

Edward Bailey recalls the last few months of the war with 86 Squadron: 'On this squadron the crew, of which I was a member, did no convoy escort duties but just flew anti U-boat patrols between the Shetland Islands and Norway. We had no sightings and I flew my last operational flight on 1 May 1945. I found the Liberator an excellent aircraft to fly in and only once in the 750 hours flying time did we have engine trouble.'

With the Atlantic, Bay of Biscay and the English Channel purged of the U-boat all that remained was to accept the surrender of these small craft, crewed by brave and daring men, who at one time had almost brought Britain to her knees. After VE Day U-boats were ordered to surface and fly a black flag in surrender. Laurie Lloyd, a second pilot in 59 Squadron recalls: 'We were on patrol on VE Day and arrived back at Ballykelly to find that everything, including the searchlight crews, were lit up. At the end of a thirteen hour 'stooge' we needed all our collective sense of humour to appreciate their high spirits. A day or so later we were sent out to pick up any surrendering U-boats. I don't know who was more surprised when we actually found one. We picked up U 1109 but were very uneasy during our first run over it. They were not sure whether we were going to be bloody-minded and drop cans on them and we couldn't be sure they were not going to let fly at us. But we passed over without incident and spent the next seven hours flying round U 1109 in tight circles until a destroyer appeared to take over escort.

'When the U-boat docked in Londonderry we went over to take a look. The souvenir hunters had been at work but the whole atmosphere inside was untidy and depressing. I finished the European part of the war feeling acutely sorry for the crews we had been trying to destroy!' In June 1945 the bomb bays were removed from most Coastal Command Liberators and their doors sealed. Canvas seats were installed and the aircraft were transfered to Transport Command for trooping flights to India.

Had more Liberators been available in sufficient quantities during the early part of the war, the U-boat menace might have been better contained. As it was, the Liberators, together with other stalwart anti-submarine aircraft like the Sunderland, Hudson and Catalina, did a magnificent job. Success might also have been greater had the Allies shown greater co-operation. For the most part, America's zone of responsibility lay in the Moroccan Sea Frontier between the two British areas—Gibraltar and West Africa. Britain's ally preferred to adopt local protection rather than send anti-submarine aircraft into the Bay of Biscay where Britain considered the U-boats most vulnerable and it was not until 1944 that effective co-operation, originally proposed by the American Secretary of War but initially rejected by both the British Cabinet and Air Vice-Marshal Slessor, was satisfactorily resolved.

U-1109 surrenders to Flying Officer Villis's Liberator of 59 Squadron based at Ballykelly, Northern Ireland.

The Big League

By the end of August 1942 over one hundred B-17s, enough for three groups, had arrived in the United Kingdom. On 17 August, the Eighth Air Force flew its first mission of the war when a handful of Fortresses were dispatched to north eastern France where they bombed a large marshalling yard. B-17 crews threw themselves headlong into a bitter war over Europe in daylight and without escort, despite opposition, particularly from the US Navy which was convinced that America's first objective lay in the defeat of Japan. In September 1942, plans to introduce the B-24

A 3rd Bomb Division Liberator overflies the blazing Daurag-Nerag crude-oil refinery which was plastered by the Eighth on 20 June 1944.

into Europe were fulfilled when the Second Bombardment Wing (which was to grow into the Second Bombardment Division and later the Second Air Division) was established in England.

Seventeen B-24D Liberators of the 93rd Bomb Group established themselves at Alconbury in Huntingdonshire. The 93rd remained in the shadow of Fortress operations for some time and it was not until 9 October 1942 that the Group flew its maiden mission, to the Fives-Lille steelworks in Belgium. This was the first mission flown by the Eighth Air Force from

East Anglia in which over a hundred bombers participated. Colonel Ted Timberlake, Commanding Officer of the 93rd and flying *Teggie Ann*, led twenty-four B-24Ds to the target behind the much larger formation of B-17s. The Group lost a B-24 over France and only ten Liberators hit their target.

At the end of the month the 93rd lost two of its squadrons on detached duty to Coastal Command, scouring the Bay of Biscay for U-boats. During October various echelons of the 44th Bomb Group equipped with B-24D Liberators arrived at Shipdham airfield in Norfolk after crossing the treacherous northern Atlantic. It fell to these two B-24 Groups and four B-17 Groups to prove conclusively that daylight precision bombing could succeed in the deadly skies over Europe. The RAF remained unconvinced and in November 1942 even American instructors doubted their crews' ability to bomb in daylight and survive against German opposition.

Experience won the hard way by the B-17 Groups and the 93rd on early missions resulted in modifications to the Liberator's armament in Northern Ireland. Fifty calibre machine-guns were installed in the vulnerable nose section to combat the head-on approach favoured by Luftwaffe fighters. Automatic belt feed systems were introduced on all machine-gun armament, replacing the cumbersome process of changing drums containing only thirty-six rounds by hand. Enterprising armament officers concocted their own field modifications, installing 'twin-fifties' in the 'glasshouse' area which were fire by bomdardiers and navigators lying on their stomachs. The Luftwaffe soon developed a healthy respect for the new armament and reverted to conventional pursuit tactics.

On 7 November 1942 the 44th Bomb Group —the 'Eightballs'—flew its first mission of the war from England when eight B-24Ds, each displaying 'Flying Eightball' emblems, flew a diversionary sweep for B-17s attacking positions in Holland. Two days later twelve B-24s of the 44th and 93rd went to Saint Nazaire in France to bomb the submarine pens. Thirty-five

Smoke canisters released from leading B-24s of the 467th are but a prelude to the clusters of bombs which are about to fall on the target at Zwiezel, Germany on 20 April 1945.

The Big League
Normal Operating Range

'Eightballs' over England. The nearest aircraft clearly shows the 'Flying Eightball' symbol while in the distance 'L', better known as the redoubtable Suzy Q, *maintains formation.*

B-17s went in first followed by the B-24s. All flew at 500 feet to avoid enemy radar, before climbing to heights ranging from 7,500 feet to 18,000 feet to bomb the target. The Fortresses suffered loss but the Liberators, bombing from 18,000 feet, were more fortunate and came through intact.

The raid confirmed that the Eighth could not attack a target from such a low level and come through unscathed. It also served to remind the planners something they had known for some time. The Liberator, with its operationally high wing loading, made it a difficult aircraft to maintain in formation above 21,000 feet although its service ceiling was put at 28,000 feet, about 4,000 feet below the optimum Fortress altitude. In addition, the B-24D's operational cruising speed of 180 mph was between ten and twenty miles per hour faster than the B-17's. This caused countless problems in mission timings and usually the Liberators were relegated to the rear of the B-17 formations and consequently soaked up all the punishment. One solution was for B-17 and B-24 missions to be flown separately and when the 93rd was transferred to North Africa to assist in operations from December 1942 until February 1943, the 44th flew separate, diversionary sweeps for the B-17 Groups. So many of these diversions were flown that the Liberator crews began to call themselves the 'Second Bombardment Diversion'.

The problem caused by the differing performance of the Liberators and the Fortresses was highlighted again on 3 January 1943 when the target was again Saint Nazaire. Eight B-24Ds from the 44th flying in the rear, accompanied sixty-eight B-17s to the submarine pens. By the time the formation had reached the target the Liberators had caught up with the B-17s and were able to bomb at a higher altitude. It was on this mission that the Eighth abandoned individual bombing in favour of Group bombing. The Liberators bombed through the Fortress formations and the practice continued on other missions to the submarine pens. Thereafter the only time B-17 crews felt safe from the weight of the B-24s' bombs was when they were on diversionary missions.

On 15 February 1943, the 44th flew another diversionary attack, this time on Dunkirk. Their target was the *Tojo*, a surface raider disguised as a slow freighter. The 67th Squadron, led by Major MacDonald, headed the formation. *Little Beaver* flew on his left wing in the number three position in the lead element. Just beneath them were three B-24s of the second element, with six more to the right and six more to the left. The formation crossed the Channel to Le Havre. MacDonald's navigator, Lieutenant 'Ben' Franklin, plotted a course to make the Germans believe that the Liberators were headed inland. However they changed direction and flew straight and level up the coast of France to Dunkirk where, three years before, the Royal Navy and an armada of small boats had rescued the British Expeditionary Force from its beaches.

But their long straight run had enabled the German gunners to determine their speed and height. From their high altitude the B-24s could release their bombs some distance out over the Channel and let their trajectory carry them in. Aboard MacDonald's Liberator the bombardier, Second Lieutenant Paul D. Caldwell, cried out 'target in view'. Arthur Cullen, the pilot, flew P. and I. for a few seconds, changing direction a few degrees right. Flak enveloped the formation and just as the bomb-release light came on at 15.40 hours, the B-24 took a direct hit.

When Cullen had recovered from the shock the Liberator was in a dive with no other ships in sight. There was no roof on the cabin, just a windshield. The cowlings were blown off number two and three engines, which were smoking. He could not operate the rudder because his leg was broken. MacDonald, sitting in the co-pilot's seat, had a bad stomach gash but signalled to bale-out. For a few moments the noseless bomber flew on, only to fall away to starboard with the port inboard engine aflame and the right inboard ripped from its mounting. Finally the starboard wing fell off and a huge explosion scattered debris among the formation, hitting another Liberator whose pilot managed to recross the Channel and force-land at Sandwich. MacDonald baled out in extreme pain, Cullen helping him by pushing him through the hole where the roof had been. He then followed MacDonald, hitting the tailplane and breaking his arm and then breaking his leg a second time. MacDonald died later in a German hospital but Cullen was eventually repatriated in September 1944 after having broken his leg a third time. Lieutenant Oliphant's B-24 was hit by flak, exploded, and was finished off by fighters. Despite all the Eightballs' endeavours the *Tojo* remained afloat.

Command experimented with another solution to the continuing problems caused by the difference in speed and altitude of the B-24 and B-17. It was decided that on the next mission, to the shipyards at Kiel, on 14 May 1943, the Liberators would fly in front of and below the Fortress formations. Some in the 44th doubted the Command decision, believing that if the B-24s slowed to the speed of the Fortresses, they would 'drop out of the sky'. Their worst fears were realized.

After assembly the 44th headed out over Cromer as the low formation at 21,000 feet. They rendezvoused some fifty miles off Cromer with a hundred plus B-17s stacked upwards to 32,000 feet. The B-24s cruised at 180 mph but they had to continuously zigzag twenty miles in one direction and forty miles in the other in order to remain behind the Fortresses. The B-24s were briefed to go over Kiel at 21,000 feet but their constant zigzagging brought them over Heligoland Bay at 18,000 feet and down to 160 mph—almost stalling speed.

The Eightballs were to have avoided the Friesian Islands but the constant zigzagging had caused them to veer off course and they crossed them at 19,000 feet and were met with sporadic bursts of flak. Major O'Brien, Commanding Officer of the 68th Squadron, observed flames emanating from the bomb-bay of the B Flight leader of 68th Squadron, piloted by Tom Holmes. The 66th Squadron flew lead, flanked by the 68th Squadron on its left and the 67th on its right and to the rear. Four B-24s of the 506th were flying their first mission in a diamond position. Tom Holmes managed to maintain height and cross the North Sea again to England. The flak had also hit the *Rugged Buggy*. O'Brien recalls: 'All of a sudden our ship was rocked by two explosions. A real indication of trouble was the manifold pressure on the two left engines which dropped to 15 psi and there was a sudden drag to the left which Howell the co-pilot, and I struggled to correct. I thought about feathering the two left engines but that would have been an invitation to the German fighters who were waiting to come in for the kill.'

Unknown to Major O'Brien flak had also blown a hole in the tail, knocking Sergeant Castillo out of his turret and amputating his foot. Three crew members in the tail came to

his aid and quickly realizing his plight pushed him out of the plane, pulling the ripcord of his parachute for him, and then they too baled out. One of the three, Sergeant Van Owen, was drowned in Kiel Bay despite wearing a Mae West. Jim O'Brien lost communication with the five men in the rear of his ship and continued to the target.

The 44th's cargo of incendiaries required a shorter trajectory and a longer bomb run than the B-17's. Flying a scattered formation the Liberators were exposed to fighter attack. Five Liberators were shot down before they had time to release their bombs. Three of these belonged to the 67th Squadron which brought up the rear of the formation. The first to go down was Lieutenant Roach and his replacement crew. There was only one survivor. Lieutenant Westbrook's Liberator had all four engines shot out over the target and went into a flat spin. Mulhausen, the engineer, and Roy Klinger, the tail gunner, were both killed. Bob Bishop the navigator, was in the nose with the bombardier, Second Lieutenant Holden R. Hayward. Bishop spotted a fighter boring in and shouted at Hayward to duck, but he did not hear him and was struck in the face by fragments and Bishop had the paint stripped from his steel helmet by the blast. The survivors proceeded to bale out. The time was just one o'clock. Westbrook picked up a parachute and baled out. Brown searched the aircraft for a parachute and he also baled out.

B-24Ds of the 44th BG bomb Dunkirk on 15 February 1943. They failed to hit the Tojo which was berthed in the port.

Bishop, meanwhile, had made his way to the nose-wheel bay where he looked out and saw a 'red carpet of tracer'. He paused for a moment until the German fighter ceased firing and then jumped. (Bishop knew the German pilot could not fire for long without his guns seizing up.) Feet up and head down in case the German should open fire on him Bishop folded his arms into 'wings' thinking it would aid his descent, but the reverse happened and he tumbled. Quickly reverting to his former position he groped for the ripcord and was horrified to discover it was not there! In his haste to leave the stricken Liberator Bishop had put his RAF chest parachute on upside-down! However he located and pulled the ripcord after free falling to about 5,000 feet to avoid being fired upon by German fighters. 'It was like standing on a motor bike doing 120 miles an hour, when suddenly a little handkerchief came out. I thought it was rather small for a parachute: then the big parachute opened out and reduced my speed to practically nil in a split second.'

Major O'Brien and the surviving members of his crew joined up with the other shot-down crews rounded up by the Germans. Bishop was landed from the Danish trawler and he and Jim O'Brien were sent to prisoner of war camps. In their absence the Eightballs were awarded the Distinguished Unit Citation for their part in the Kiel raid, the first such award made to an Eighth Air Force Group. After the Kiel raid there was serious talk of sending home all flying men who had completed fifteen missions. However, their experience was considered vital and they remained on active service.

On 29 May the 44th and a few 93rd Liberators, hastily withdrawn from night operations to bolster the flagging fortunes of the 'Eightballs', were taken off operations. The B-17 crews thought their friends in the Liberator crews had suffered so unmercifully that they were being withdrawn from the ETO altogether. However, they were not witnessing the break-up of the Liberator force but withdrawal for training missions for the Ploesti raid. In early June they were joined by the

389th—'Sky Scorpions'—fresh from America. After a series of raids in support of the 'Torch' operation Ploesti was attacked from Libya on 1 August. When the three Groups returned to England later that month they were confronted with a new breed of Liberator, the B-24H and J with power operated nose turrets belonging to the 392nd Bomb Group at Wendling.

This fourth B-24 Group heralded a new era for the Liberator in Europe and was soon joined by the 445th, 446th, 448th, and 453rd Groups, all equipped with the 'H' and 'J' models. Even so the Division was still not strong enough to mount deep penetration raids without fighter escort. The 445th was still not quite operational when on 13 December 1943 it was ordered to prepare for its first mission. Less than one month after landing in Norfolk fifteen aircraft took off from Tibenham and joined with the Division for a raid on Kiel. Despite heavy flak the 445th returned without loss and all twelve crews hit the target. It was a quite remarkable effort. Three days later the 446th also flew its first mission of the war when it joined in an attack on Bremen.

On 1 December, the 448th's ground echelon had arrived in Norfolk, but it was not until the 22nd that the Group was ready for its first operational mission, when it joined with groups of the Division for a raid on Osnabruck, Germany. It was the Group's first taste of combat and Sergeant Sheehan recalls the mission clearly: 'Osnabruck turned out to be heavily defended. Although flak was minimal the fighters were there in abundance as we found out. My first encounter with combat commenced with black puffs of flak dotting the sky around us. It was something we never did get accustomed to. The effectiveness of this was shown when part of a ship began trailing smoke and parachutes. As we approached the target the aircraft to our immediate right began dropping bombs. At the moment it occurred I could not believe my eyes. I thought it could not be happening at all. The aircraft leading this box formation dropped its entire bomb load on the left wing of one of its wing men's

Below: Liberators of the 458th parade on the Horsham St. Faith taxiways like circus elephants, brakes squealing, noses bobbing up and down and rudders flapping like ears.

Right: The vital Nazi oil refineries at Politz, Germany are hit by formations of Liberators of the 8th Air Force on 20 June 1944. A large cloud of oily black smoke curls its way heavenward as the effect of the unleashing of the lethal load is felt on the target below.

Inset: A waist-gunner's eye view of a Liberator flying through heavy flak over Germany.

Lt Karl W. Ruthenbeck's B-24J of the 492nd BG crosses the Schulau oil refinery during the group's penultimate mission on 6 August 1944.

On 24 February the Second Bomb Division went to the ME110 assembly plant at Gotha. A force of 235 Liberators crossed the Dutch coast.

Flak was heavy over Lingen and the Liberators encountered persistent attacks by the Luftwaffe. Even the arrival of three Thunderbolt Groups just after 12.00 hours was unable to prevent five Liberators from the 445th being shot down in the space of six minutes. Over 150 enemy fighters ferociously attacked the formation all the way to the target despite close attention from escorting fighters. The Division beat off incessant attacks as it flew on over the Dummer Lake where it veered south-eastwards to Osnabruck and the bombed-out airfields near Hanover. Three more 445th B-24s were shot down before the formation turned south near Gottingen at 12.53 hours. Nine minutes later a 445th B-24 belonging to the 703rd Squadron was shot down.

P-47 Thunderbolts had escorted the Liberators to the vicinity of Hanover and then the twin-boomed P-38 Lightnings and P-51 Mustangs orbited the formation as it proceeded to Gotha. Undaunted, FW-190s, ME-110s, ME-210s, and JU-88s raked the American formations with cannon- and rocket-fire. Using the Liberators' thick vapour trails to excellent advantage, they often struck at any lagging bomber from below and behind. The Luftwaffe even attempted to disrupt the large and unwieldly combat wings.

At 13.09 hours the Division changed course to the south-east with a feint towards Meinegen. Some confusion arose at the I.P. when the navigator in the 389th lead ship suffered oxygen failure and veered off course. The bombardier slumped over his sight and accidentally tripped the bombs. Altogether twenty-five Liberators bombed the secondary target at Eisenach. Before the small 445th formation reached the target its tenth and eleventh victims fell to the German guns. By now the 445th consisted of only fourteen Liberators, three having aborted before entering Germany. Another 445th machine was shot down just after leaving Eisenach.

The thirteen remaining 445th B-24s, realizing that they had veered off course, continued alone. They arrived over the target at 13.25 hours and executed an eight-minute bomb run. Some 180 500-pounders dropped from 12,200 feet inflicted considerable damaged on the Gotha plant. Other Second Bombardment Division Groups, totalling 171 Liberators dropped another 468 tons of assorted bombs from varying altitudes and directions. The 445th's thirteenth B-24 fell victim to the German defences minutes after bombs away.

The plant's destruction was well received by Eighth Bomber Command who estimated that six to seven weeks' production would be lost. However, seven B-24s from the 392nd were missing, thirteen landed with varying degrees of damage and other groups too had suffered.

aircraft that had drifted down and under him. Stunned I watched the damaged aircraft fade left and over on its back. I prayed for 'chutes to appear, but none did. I was brought back to reality by the call over the intercom, "Fighters!" At this point everything seemed unreal and I guess I was doing things purely automatically and practically as I had been taught.

'Twin-engined enemy aircraft were lobbing rockets into a formation of bombers to my right. At first they seemed oblivious to our presence. I commenced firing at one of the fighters, which began trailing smoke and fire and went down through the clouds. I was later given credit for this kill. (To receive credit for downing an enemy ship it must be confirmed by the aircraft directly behind you.)' The Division lost thirteen Liberators that day.

The New Year began with the famous General Jimmy Doolittle taking over command of the Eighth Air Force on 1 January 1944. His directive was simple: 'Win the air war and isolate the battlefield!' In other words: 'Destroy the Luftwaffe and cut off the Normandy beaches for the Invasion.' At Squadron and Group level the men under his command were impressed. They all felt they knew the famous American aviator, not only from his aeroplane racing days but from his leading the famous B-25 raid on Tokyo.

The 445th alone lost 122 men on the bloody mission.

By March 1944 the Second Bombardment Division had grown to eleven groups with the addition of three new groups, the 458th, 466th, and 467th, making up the 96th Combat Wing. The future looked bright for the Liberator in the ETO but the Eighth's commanders now found themselves with more Liberator groups than they needed. During April five B-24 groups landed in England and despite the obvious drawbacks of mixing two types of heavy bomber, they joined the Third Bombardment Division, hitherto equipped with the Fortress. Doolittle had wanted to bring the Eighth up to strength with Fortresses but there were simply not enough to go round. In contrast, by the late spring of 1944, five B-24 plants in America were producing more than enough Liberators.

The uneasy marriage between the Fortress and Liberator in the Third Bombardment Division ended only four months later. From July to September all five Third Bombardment Division Liberator groups were converted to Fortresses. During the last fortnight of July the 486th and 487th Bomb Groups, which formed the 92nd CBW, were taken off operations and by the end of the month were ready to begin combat operations with the B-17. Between the end of August and mid-September the three groups belonging to the 93rd CBW, the 34th, 490th and 493rd, also changed to the Fortress. At first crews resented the change-over but they quickly grew to like the improved flying characteristics inherent in the B-17 and praised the more spacious nose compartment and improved heating. Meanwhile, the discarded B-24Hs and Js were sent to depots for modification and overhaul and many found their way into Second Bombardment Division groups anxious to replace severe losses sustained in the large number of missions flown in the months preceding D-Day.

On D-Day itself, every available aircraft was mobilized to fly support missions for the invasion.

The first mission was primarily concerned with the neutralizing of enemy coastal defences and front-line troops. Subsequent missions were directed against lines of communication leading to the bridgehead. The Liberators would be in good company with no less than thirty-six Squadrons of Mustangs and Thunderbolts patrolling the area. Initially they would protect the bombers but would later break off and strafe ground targets. It was evident that there could be no delay and that stragglers would be left to their fate. Any aborts were to drop out of the formation before leaving the English coast and then fly back to base at below 14,000 feet. It was a one-way aerial corridor and the traffic flow intense. If a B-24 had to be ditched, only those ships returning to England from the beach-head would stop to pick up the crews. Finally, new

instructions on prisoner-of-war procedures were given. General Doolittle, in a message read out to the men at all bases, said: 'The Eighth Air Force is currently charged with a most solemn obligation in support of the most vital operation ever undertaken by our armed forces. . . .'

Briefing over, a line of trucks was assembled to take the crews to their waiting Liberators. At 01.30 hours the slumbering Cathedral city of Norwich and the pre-dawn calm of the surrounding countryside were shattered by the roar of thousands of Twin Wasps being pre-flighted at all points of the compass. Overhead the moon shone through thick black undercast.

At Hardwick, Bob Shaffer was one of the many who had spent all night in careful preparation: 'We took off at 14.00 hours. The flak was light and the mission successful. I flew as lead bombardier in *Naughty Nan* piloted by Lieutenant Sneddon. There was a full moon and I have never seen as many ships of all descriptions as there were crossing the Channel. I saw battleships firing at gun emplacements. It was quite a sight—quite a show.'

The final cog of 20th Wing, the 448th, also joined the formation. Ben Isgrig recalls: 'It was just getting light as our formation left the English coast and the clouds broke enough for us to see the hundreds of ships in the Channel

Incendiary clusters cascade from Liberators of the 93rd BG during the greatest daylight raid made on Berlin on 18 March 1945.

heading for France. We could plainly see the heavy warships shelling the coast, which was shrouded in smoke. Besides seeing more ships than I had ever seen before, there were also more heavy bombers in the air than I thought possible to put up in one area. The coast itself was covered in clouds. We didn't see our target at all; neither did we see flak or fighters.'

Meanwhile the 96th Wing was *en route* to its target on the French coast. It flew in elements of six aircraft. One ship in each element was equipped with H2X to locate targets if they were obscured. Their inclusion was prudent because complete overcast during the mission was to prove disastrous. Many Squadrons were joined by Liberators from other groups who had strayed off course and only sixteen B-24s of the 467th managed to drop their bombs. Only about half of the 264 500-pounders and only about a third of the 100-pounders were released over the targets. The crews were bitterly disappointed.

There was no sleep for those left behind. A second mission was being planned and this to be followed by a third. Ground crews earned no respite and after a hasty breakfast they were out again working on the aircraft. Ironically, amid all the activity, the German radio at Calais was on the air playing a song called 'Invasion Day'.

Some crews were required to fly their second mission of the day, as was Ben Isgrig: 'Instead of being excited, as we had been in the morning, we were just tired and worn out.

Again we saw the landing-craft in the Channel; again our target [Caen] was covered by clouds. We saw no flak or fighters.'

The second D-Day mission was very discouraging. A small formation joined with the 96th Wing in an attack on Villers Breage, France. The Liberators had a good tailwind all the way but apart from that the weather was against them. They ran into overcast and at about 05.50 hours thick clouds drifted over the target forcing crews to release bombs using radar. A slight improvement was made on the third mission, flown that afternoon, when overcast still draped its cloudy curtain all the way from England to the invasion coast.

The Liberators did succeed in disrupting communications and damaging airfields while the flow of Allied troops into the bridgehead continued unabated. It was a superb effort by both the ground and air crews. Many airmen flew more than fifteen hours and went without sleep for thirty hours.

A total of 2,362 B-24 and B-17 sorties were flown by the Eighth on D-Day. The only heavy bomber to be lost to enemy action was a Liberator of the 487th from Lavenham.

On 7 August the 492nd was withdrawn from combat after losing fifty-four aircraft between May and July 1944. This was the heaviest loss of any Liberator group for a three-month period. Crews were dispersed throughout the rest of the Eighth. The 491st, late of the 45th CBW, took over at North Pickenham, the 492nd's previous base, and began operations

with the 14th CBW. The 491st's former 45th CBW partner, the 489th, was transferred to the 20th CBW. The Second Bombardment Division now totalled an unlucky thirteen groups and remained that number until November 1944 when the 489th was rotated Stateside, on paper at least, for redeployment to the Pacific as a B-29 outfit.

Meanwhile, on 28 August the 20th Wing groups had been converted to a transportation role in support of the Allied ground forces in France, who were in urgent need of fuel and supplies. On 29 August the 93rd, 446th, and 448th commenced 'trucking' missions, as they were called. Crew chiefs stopped painting bomb symbols on the Liberators and instead stencilled flour sacks and freight cars. They flew empty to the depot in southern England where Royal Artillerymen loaded the cavernous Liberators which stood in long rows. These missions continued until 9 September. But when the Allies launched 'Operation Market Garden' using British and American airborne division against German-held Dutch towns on the Rhine in mid-September, the Liberators were once again called upon to supplement the troop carriers.

British troops landed at Arnhem and American forces at Eindhoven and Nijmegen in an attempt to secure a foothold on the east bank of the Rhine. It was planned to cut off the German Army in the Belgian sector and save the bridges and the port of Antwerp for the advancing ground forces. It was also hoped

Left Top: *A tight formation of 93rd BG Liberators releases bombs on enemy installations on a D-Day support mission.*

Left Centre: *A 486th BG Liberator passes over allied shipping off the Normandy beach-head near Caen on D-Day 6 June 1944.*

Left Bottom: *The Worry Bird of the 446th BG during a break in missions.*

Centre: *Waco gliders litter I.Z. N near Knapheide. The First Allied Airborne Army recovered 80 per cent of all supplies dropped by the 20th Wing at DZ.N, Knapheide-Klein Amerika (Little America) near Groesbeek.*

Right Top: *Parachutes attached to supply canisters billow out over the Best during the 44th's contribution to 'Operation Market Garden' on 18 September 1944.*

Right Below: *Captain Jim Hunter's lead ship from the 491st BG was brought down on the supply mission of 18 September 1944. It hit the haystack (bottom right of picture) and exploded. Only the tail-gunner survived.*

that the operation would draw the Germans away from Aachen. For an operation of this size, the Liberators' involvement was crucial. Fuel for the Allied armour and transport was in short supply.

The 458th began its 'trucking' operations on 12 September, delivering just over 13,000 gallons of fuel to units in France. It was then stood down until the night of the 17th. During the day groups from the 14th and 20th Wings flew practice 'trucking' missions over Norfolk. That night motor trucks brought supplies to the bases in the region and men loaded each Liberator with about 6,000 lb of perishables and fuel supplies. Altogether 252 supply-carrying B-24s took off for France on the first full Divisional 'trucking' mission on 18 September, including six specially modified 458th Liberators, deliverying over 9,000 gallons

of fuel to General Patton's forces. During September, in thirteen days of flying 'trucking' missions, the 458th delivered 727,160 gallons of fuel to France.

On 27 September the Second Bomb Division put up 315 Liberators, including thirty-seven from the 445th, to raid the Henschel engine and vehicle assembly plants at Kassel in central Germany. Low cloud dogged the mission and visibility was poor. The 445th, navigating by Gee, made a miscalculation at the I.P. and headed for Göttingen, about thirty miles to the north-east of Kassel. Major Heaton, one of the 453rd lead pilots, noticed the 445th heading off to the left in the wrong direction and he immediately checked with his lead navigator who advised him that the 453rd was on course for the target. Heaton immediately attempted to call the 445th lead pilot but the radios were not communicating clearly and the 445th was, at the time, almost out of range.

The 445th dropped its bombs through solid cloud and they fell half a mile short of Göttingen. It then swung farther to the east placing the group well behind the main force. Major Heaton watched as they headed into an area where the Luftwaffe was forming for an attack. The 445th flew on for another ten minutes when, a few mile from Eisenach, more than a hundred enemy fighters, exploiting the clouds to excellent advantage, swooped down on the Liberators in lines of three abreast. The Focke-Wulfs appeared at six o'clock followed by two Gruppen of ME-109s. The fighters, some flying ten abreast, opened fire immediately.

In a very few minutes the sky was a holocaust with twenty-five burning Liberators falling to earth. Many more received serious damage. The sky seemed to be raining parachutes. Even the intervention of the 361st Group's Mustangs was not enough to save the

445th although, in a brief battle, they did shoot down several German fighters. Two 445th Liberators crash-landed in France, a third managed to cross the Channel only to crash in Kent, while a fourth crashed near Tibenham. Only seven aircraft made it back to the airfield and they carried one dead crewman and thirteen wounded.

Losses within the Liberator groups continued to rise and on 25 November the 491st lost sixteen Liberators in almost as many minutes during a mission to the oil-refineries at Misburg. With the German breakthrough in the Ardennes on 16 December 1944, missions intensified in support of the Battle of the Bulge. East Anglia was still in the grip of a particularly bleak December and it was not until Christmas Eve that the fog lifted sufficiently for the Eighth to mount its long awaited strike. A record 2,034 bombers, including war-weary hacks and even assembly ships, took off on the largest single strike flown by the Allied Air Forces of the war. A smaller force was dispatched on Christmas Day but such was the urgency of the situation that another raid was ordered for 29 December. Runways were covered with ice and snow, and fog added to the treacherous conditions. Despite this Command decided that the mission in support of General Patton's forces near Metz was so imperative that it must go ahead. At Rackheath, near Norwich, the 467th managed to get four Liberators off on instruments before Colonel Shower, the Commanding Officer, cancelled the mission. One Liberator touched a tree on take-off and managed to land at nearby Attlebridge. Another crew baled out after heading their bomber out to sea while the other two crashed, one on top of the other.

On New Year's Day 1945 the Second Bombardment Division was redesignated the Second Air Division and the Liberators returned to the strategic offensive with a raid on Koblenz. Meanwhile, many ground staff on the East Anglian bases were transferred to the flagging infantry fighting in the Ardennes and disabled and injured men arrived to take their place. All at once the 'general bitching' ceased as many realized how much better off they had been than their counterparts in France. Missions continued, weather permitting, and in March 1945 the Second Air Division Liberators were once again called upon to drop supplies, this time to Field-Marshal Bernard Montgomery's Second Army crossing the Rhine at Wesel. Approximately 6,000 aircraft of all types took part in the operation and the murderous ground-fire accounted for many of the fourteen Liberators that failed to return. One hundred and four Liberators returned to their bases damaged in one way or another.

Throughout the remainder of March and early April ME262 jet fighters were seen regularly by Liberator crews. Fortunately, their incursions were kept to a minimum by lack of fuel and a shortage of pilots to fly the

revolutionary fighter. The Eighth retaliated by bombing their airfields, but only the end of the war ended their threat completely.

The end came on 25 April 1945 when the Second Air Division Liberators bombed four rail complexes surrounding Hitler's mountain retreat at Berchtesgaden. Groups then flew 'Trolley' missions over western Europe so that ground crews could witness at first hand the destruction their Liberators had wrought. From the middle of May to the end of July all thirteen Second Air Division Liberator groups returned to America via Wales and the Azores.

During operations, the Division lost 1,458 Liberators and 6,032 airmen killed, flying a total of 95,948 sorties on 493 operational missions. The Division was awarded six Presidential Unit Citations and five individuals received the Medal of Honor.

A 389th BG Liberator trails fire 300 feet long and begins to break up after being hit in the fuel tanks during a raid on Munster.

Ploesti

The greatest single source of fuel for the German war machine in all Europe was the oil refinery complex at Ploesti in Rumania. To bomb it and destroy it would be a great morale booster for the Allies. As the British Eighth Army retreated into Egypt and the situation in the Middle East deteriorated it was decided to make a strike on Ploesti. Only one heavy bomber had the nescessary range—the B-24D Liberator—and even that would be operating at its absolute extreme because from the North African coast to Ploesti is over 1100 miles.

The only Liberators available were twenty-three unsuspecting B-24Ds *en route* to China, commanded by Colonel Harry A. Halverson.

Between 22.30 and 23.00 hours on 11 June thirteen Liberators of the 'Halverson Detachment', codenamed HALPRO took off from Fayid, Egypt and proceeded individually to Ploesti. At dawn on the morning of 12 June they arrived over the refineries and began their bombing runs. Ten hit the Astra Romana Refinery while one B-24D blasted the port of Constanta and another two released their bombs on unidentified targets. Results were in proportion to the number of aircraft despatched. One oil depot was destroyed and the port of Constanta damaged but Ploesti had been raided and American heavy bombers had bombed a European target for the first time.

Although no Liberators were shot down on the mission, indeed there was no serious fighter opposition, all thirteen Liberators were forced to land in neutral countries. Colonel Halverson and six other pilots landed in Iraq and two others put down in Syria. *Brooklyn Rambler, Blue Goose, Little Eva* and *Edna Elizabeth* landed in Turkey although the *Rambler* took off again some months later when its pilot Lieutenant Nathan J Brown escaped!

The HALPRO detachment remained in Egypt and on the morning of 15 June seven of its B-24Ds joined with two Liberators of No. 160 (RAF) Squadron in a raid against Axis shipping in the Mediterranean. More HALPRO raids from the Middle East followed and despite Colonel Halverson (now returned from Iraq) requesting permission to proceed to China the remnants of the Detachment remained in the Middle East and in July 1942 reformed into the First Provisional Bomb Group. Four months later the First Provisional Group became the 376th Bomb Group, better known as the 'Liberandos'. In July 1942 they were joined by the 98th Bomb Group, which arrived in the Middle East from America, and was based in Palestine. Its B-24Ds had been painted in 'Desert Pink', more popularly known to crews as 'Titty Pink'. Both groups flew missions in support of the Eighth Army and in 1943, further afield to targets in Sicily and Southern Italy.

In the summer of 1943 the American air forces turned again to the Ploesti oil complex. This time the HALPRO detachment and the

The Sandman *of the 98th BG banks over the blazing inferno of Ploesti.*

B-24D Liberators of the 'Halverson Detachment' over Egypt.

mess tins when jokers 'accidentally' kicked the tent stakes. Other reptiles abounded and the generic term 'grampers' was coined—one 389th crew actually named their B-24 *The Little Gramper*. For the more aggressive men there was usually a kangaroo rat chase in the cool of the evening. These comic-looking raiding parties, wearing only khaki shorts ran all over the desert chasing the creatures with sticks. The other favourite pastime was crushing grasshoppers with a stick after supper.

At night the cold was intense. Men slept on a cot inside a mattress cover with two blankets but these did little to maintain warmth. During the daylight hours the heat was interminable and the sand permeated everything, including food, men's hair and shoes, and aircraft engines. The only water available came from a chemically treated Lister bag which hung all day in the sun.

For three weeks the groups flew support missions for the Italian campaign, bombing Italian and Mediterranean targets. On 20 June they began twelve days' training for Ploesti, with practice flights against a mock-up target in the desert. The crews of most of the Liberator groups were apprehensive. This was no ordinary mission and morale was not helped when General Brereton, who was in overall command of 'Operation Statesman' told crews that losses were expected to be as high as fifty per cent. The momentous mission was scheduled for 1 August 1943.

98th were joined by three Eighth Air Force groups from East Anglia. The 44th and 93rd had already tasted combat over Europe, but the 389th—'The Sky Scorpions'—had only arrived in England some two months previously.

Low level training flights were made over East Anglia, much to the chagrin of the crews, trained in the art of high altitude precision bombing. Hedge-hopping was alien to them and, not surprisingly, accidents happened. On 25 June two Liberators of the inexperienced 389th were involved in a mid-air collision. One man was killed and another seriously injured. During the last week of June 1943 the three groups, totalling 124 aircraft, left England for the Libyan desert.

Conditions on the bases were primitive and were not helped by the Ninth Air Force who provided all the Eighth's rations. All ranks queued outside the mess tent for powdered eggs, spam, dehydrated potatoes and powdered lemonade, while the best rations were put aside by the Ninth Air Force groups until after the Eighth had returned to England.

Thousands of grasshoppers hung on the underside of the mess tent and dropped into

Crews were briefed the night before the raid as it was barely daylight the following morning when the Liberators took off. The Ninth Air Force's 376th BG led the raid. Behind them came the 93rd, then the 98th, followed by the 44th and 389th bringing up the rear. Twenty-nine Liberators from the 389th took off from Benghazi around six o'clock in the morning. Altogether 358 men from the Group went on the mission, some flying with the 98th on detached service. Each 389th Liberator carried four five-hundred pound bombs and full fuel tanks, including an additional 400 gallon tank in the bomb bay.

The five Liberator groups formed and headed out over the Mediterranean. Earl Zimmerman, flying with Lieutenant James's crew, recalls: 'Three planes were lost before we even got to the target. One of them carried the lead navigator and it came down in the Mediterranean. We crossed over the spot and saw black smoke coming up. One crashed on take-off and we lost another over land.'

It was a beautiful blue summer's day and the Liberators headed for the island of Corfu, then veered right, to the east, heading over land to Ploesti. As crews crossed the Danube they looked down at the peaceful scene where some barges were floating near the shore. The Liberators approached their target around 14.00 hours. A few clouds dotted the area but it was still a bright, sunny day. From this point events

Men of the 389th BG enjoying the fruits of their labours at Benghazi in August 1943.

began to overtake the B-24s. The leading 376th mistook the I.P. and turned south too soon and the 93rd followed. The 389th reached their check point at Pitesti and veered north east. The target 389th sought was the Steaua Romana refinery at Campina. It was thought to be an easier target compared with those of the other groups because it had no barrage balloons. Up to this moment the formation had not encountered any flak or fighters. Some Fortresses flew a diversion off the coast of Italy which may have helped their Liberator colleagues. The 'Sky Scorpions' had been allocated the longest route because their Liberators were the only ones fitted with fuselage tanks. However, this additional weight made them very vulnerable.

Earl Zimmerman recalls: 'We were made to drain the gas gauges on the flight deck prior to taking off because they figured that if we got hit by ground fire it would be less likely to catch fire. Just before we hit the target our pilot got a little worried about the gas consumption because we were flying in the last element. Flying in the tail end of the formation you always used more fuel because you were constantly jockeying the controls. It takes a bit more manoeuvring to stay in formation and we were constantly being buffeted by prop wash. We were really burning up the gas. The engineer told me that if we had turned round then we could not have made Benghazi! We knew we were not going back no matter what happened over the target.'

The 389th's Commanding Officer, Colonel Jack Wood, led the 'Sky Scorpions' in Major Kenneth 'Fearless' Caldwell's Liberator. There were some anxious moments when the formation turned down the wrong valley. The group pulled up and flew on for perhaps three to four minutes before turning to the right. They started down towards the refinery, which was marked by a great pall of smoke. The 389th carried bombs with only ten-second delay fuses while the other groups carried twenty-minute acid core fused bombs which would not explode until the bombs dropped by the 389th created a concussion wave in the target area. Any that did not explode in the concussion wave would eventually explode by means of the acid core fuse.

After the 389th made the wrong turn going in the Group split into three sections and hit the target from three different directions. The 'Sky Scorpions' totally destroyed the Campina refinery; the only group to achieve total destruction of their target. But the destruction was not achieved without cost. Lieutenant Lloyd D. Hughes and Lieutenant Horton went down over the target. Lloyd Hughes was posthumously awarded the Medal of Honor after pressing home his attack despite being holed time and again. Blazing fuel finally engulfed his B-24 which hit the ground and exploded. Altogether nine Liberators from the

389th failed to return to North Africa. The 'Sky Scorpions' had been the last to arrive over the target area and had paid dearly for their lack of surprise. When Lieutenant James's Liberator came off the target the only B-24 in front, which the crew could see was *Hitler's Hearse*, flown by Captain Mooney of the Eighth's 567th Squadron. Second Lieutenant James F. Gerrits, the co-pilot aboard *Hitler's Hearse*, takes up the story:

'As we started down and saw the target, Bob Mooney was all excited. He said to me, "There it is, get those nose guns firing Hank!" (We had two 0.50 calibre guns specially mounted in the nose for shooting up the target a little and mostly to demoralize the ground gunners.) I had a toggle switch to fire them and I flipped it a couple of times and heard them roar. We headed down on a long glide into the target. There were a lot of orange blips appearing all over from around the target area. We looked down the barrels of the guns as they were firing at us. Everything was fine and then suddenly there was a loud bang in the cockpit. It quickly filled with smoke. I flinched away and turned toward my side window. As the smoke cleared

Major-General Lewis H. Brereton addresses the 'Liberandos' near Benghazi in July 1943. Although he expected losses to be up to fifty per cent, Brereton felt that if the Ploesti oilfields were hit it would be worth it. Brereton was ordered by General Hap Arnold not to go on the mission.

Liberators flying low in formation on their way to attack the oil refineries at Ploesti. Taken from a Liberator of the 389th.

there was a horrible roar from a hole in the windscreen and I turned toward Mooney. He was leaning back, away from the control wheel. His hands were off the wheel and just held in front of him. Blood was running all down his face. It was evident right away that he wasn't conscious anymore. We were still going down on the target in a shallow dive and maybe 200 feet or so off the ground. I quickly grabbed the wheel and held the run for a few seconds. Then I pulled up and to the right and we went over the refinery structures a little to the right. I could feel something down the side of my face and my left arm hurt. I looked down and I had some blood on myself too.

'The air was roaring in through the hole and the windshield where the shell had entered just to the left of Mooney's head. I was alone. Garret, the engineer, had disappeared too. I thought it was all over for us so I felt we should give them hell before we crashed. I pushed my intercom button and shouted, "O.K. now give it to them, pour it at 'em. Let's go now. Keep those guns going!" I was talking to the tail gunner and the ball turret gunner, who had good shots at the refinery as we were pulling away. Then we were low over the trees, past the target and still in the air.

'I tried to get just a little more altitude but I was too shaken to do much of anything but just fly. My engineer, Charles Garret, had been standing back between Mooney and me and had been hit around the head and hands. He got up between us to show us his bleeding hands and I yelled, "Garret, get him (Mooney) out of his seat, get him out anyway you can—pull his clothes off!"

'Garret got him out and laid him on the flight deck just behind the cockpit. We flew on and Garret climbed into Mooney's seat to help me but he couldn't do very much. His hands had

been hit and were all bloody. He pushed the controls with just the palms of his hands. Somebody called over the intercom that number three engine was smoking badly. J. D. Wilson, the navigator, called very excitedly, "If you don't feather that engine now you'll never feather it." I said to Garret to go ahead and feather it. But Garret really didn't know how to and the the engine ran away a couple of times. It really raced and roared but he finally did get it stopped.

'We found out that we had lost all the controls to engine number four as well and we couldn't do anything about it except let it run the way it was set. I asked Garret, "How is Mooney?" By then Spencer one of the waist gunners, had come forward to help and he was working over Mooney. Then Garret turned to me and said, "Spencer says Mooney is dead." That was a blow but I had to act tough and say, "Well, O.K. let's keep going."

'I called my bombardier, Rock Triantafellu, and said, "Rock, dump the bombs anywhere. Get rid of them." But he said they had been dropped on the target. Rock came up from the nose just as I was passing over a cleared area of land, I was still all shook up and I said, "Rock, should I land on that flat ground right down there?" I pointed at the field. But he said, "No, No, keep it in the air for a while." Leibowitz, the top turret gunner, had been hit too and he came out of his turret to the flight deck. But Rock, when he saw him, said "Leibowitz, get back up there and get that turret turning." Rock went back down to the nose again and then J. D. Wilson, the navigator, came up. He had a really horrified look on his face when he saw me and the mess on the flight deck. There was blood all over the wounded and the dead. Leuben, the radio-operator, had also been hit pretty bad and was lying on the floor too.

Broken glass was everywhere and the air was roaring in through the front. It didn't look like we could possibly keep going.

'Leuben asked, "What are you going to do?" I said, "Go to Czechoslovakia and bale out I guess." (We had been alerted that the partisans were waiting for us between two towns in Czechoslovakia in case we did have to go there.) J.D. went back down to the nose. Rock told me later that when he got there he had buckled on a knapsack to his parachute harness and had begun pulling open the nose-wheel door which was an emergency exit. Rock said to him, "What are you doing J.D.?" J.D. answered, "I'm getting out of here, we're going to crash." But Rock told him, "J.D. we're only a hundred or so feet up and besides that's your knapsack you have buckled on; not your parachute!" J.D. quieted down some and took off the knapsack.

'We decided to head for Turkey since we had a map showing an airport at Izmir. We thought we might cross Turkey and get down to Cyprus which was under British control. J.D. got back to work and gave me a compass heading for Izmir. Then Rock told me we were getting low on gas. We had been hit by a big shell in the bomb bay tank and in spite of a thick rubber lining that was supposed to seal those leaks, almost all 400 gallons had leaked out quickly. Rock had seen it and had jammed an A-2 leather flight jacket into the hole but it had just washed the jacket right out and the gas kept on going. Garret ordinarily did the gas, transferring with a pump from tank to tank but he was too badly wounded so Rock had to do it. He transferred gas from the engine that wasn't running to the other tank. But he didn't work it just right with the pump and got a couple of facefuls of gas. It burned his face and he couldn't see very well.

'The rest of our flight didn't know what was going on so Rock went back to the waist window to signal them. Our radio had been shot out but in any event we wanted to maintain radio silence so as not to attract attention. Rock signalled with an Aldis lamp to one wingship, "Mooney's dead, Going to Turkey." We kept on flying and I increased the power. We were climbing very slowly with our one dead engine but got up to 6,000 feet. We went too near one town and we drew flak. I quickly veered away and our wingships followed. Two twin-engined JU 88s came at us from a distance but for some reason they broke off without attacking.

'By now J.D., Rock and I had figured that we would go down the coast of Turkey as far as we could until the gas ran out. We finally came to the Bosphorus but it became so hazy that I had to go on instruments again and we worked our way down over the mountains to Izmir. I let down a little on this leg. When we were near Izmir I told Rock to put down the landing gear using the hand emergency system since the hydraulic lines had been ruptured. We figured by then we were so low on gas we couldn't go any further than Izmir. We had no flaps or brakes either so it was going to be a difficult landing. Rock got the gear down and then we had another problem. With the drag of the gear I couldn't maintain altitude. We gradually dropped. J.D. brought me right to the airport. I went over it and then tried to turn. But I was afraid to bank too much with the engine out. We lost altitude and flying at low air speed I lost the airport in the slow turn.

'I was almost frantic. We were in a valley between two mountain ranges. By then we could only go on up the valley. I yelled, "Where is the airport?" But everybody was numb by that time and nobody answered. I said, "Throw

Far Left: *A series of photographs taken during and after the Ploesti raid, from a Liberator of the 389th.*

Left Top: *Colonel Compton and Brigadier General Ent prepare to take off for Ploesti in the command ship Teggie Ann.*

Left Bottom: *Liberators race over the Northern African desert at tree top height during training for the raid on Ploesti. A mock-up target was built in the desert and bombed with 100 lb delayed action bombs.*

Above Left: *A Liberator of the 98th BG roars over the Astra Romana Refinery amid smoke and flame. The Pyramiders suffered the highest casualties of all five groups, losing twenty-one of the thirty-eight B-24s that started out from North Africa. At least nine were destroyed by the blasts from delayed action bombs dropped by the 376th.*

Above Right: *Colonel Jack Wood, Commanding Officer of the 389th.*

41

everything out to reduce our rate of descent." And the crew did toss various stuff out. By then there were also two Turkish P-40 fighters buzzing around us and diving at us to force us down. But we were in too much trouble and too busy and exhausted to pay any attention at all to them. I didn't know what to do. We kept going and finally I saw a big grazing field below us on the left. We were maybe 400 or 500 feet up so I started to turn to the left. But I couldn't push the rudder pedal on the left far enough. In desperation I put both feet on the left rudder and skidded around 270 degrees.

'After I got around the turn I saw the field directly in front of me and I pulled the throttles off watching the air speed as well as I could. No flaps, so we came in real hot. At the last minute, right in front of me, loomed an irrigation ditch. I thought for a second in frustration of just ploughing through it but that would have been disastrous. I grabbed all the throttles and jammed them forward. The engines roared, the left wing dropped and we picked up enough altitude to clear the ditch. I pulled the throttles back as quickly as I had pushed them forward and grabbed the wheel with both hands, struggling furiously to bring the left wing up and to flatten out the glide. We touched down and the potholes were real rough. We were far too fast and we bounced back up, made a slow glide, then touched down again. The second time it was really rough. We tore along with no brakes and I was jamming the controls one way and then the other to try to ground loop. But we kept rolling straight ahead. Then I saw another irrigation gulley at the far edge of the field and I thought we were going to nose into it for sure. But we slowed down and I shouted, "Hang on, we're going in." But we rolled on up to the edge. The nosewheel was right on the brink but we stopped.

'We all climbed out quickly through the bomb bays and carried out the dead and wounded. We were all so uptight we talked, shouted and walked around. Then somebody mentioned the secret radio equipment. But the gas fumes in *Hitler's Hearse* made me afraid to push the destruction buttons. I went back into the aircraft through the waist window. One of the crew pointed out the radio equipment to me and I shot at it with my .45 pistol.

'It was a tremendous relief to be on the ground but I couldn't quieten down. I could only walk around and around the plane. I looked up at that huge engine dripping oil and the big prop with the strangely unnatural feathered attitude. One of the Turkish pilots landed his P-40 behind us but it had much smaller wheels than the Liberator and he tore the gear and one wing off. He got out safely and walked across a couple of hundred yards to us. He was very pleasant and gave all of us a cigarette. The sun was just going down behind the mountain. It was about 18.30 and it was a beautiful clear quiet evening, with just some

sheep grazing in the field nearby. A little later a Turkish army truck came up with a few soldiers in it and loaded all of us up and took us to a little hamlet a mile or so away. Some sort of first-aid man there cleaned and dressed our wounds. By then it was dark and the truck took us into Izmir. Mooney lay on the floor of the truck, covered with some jackets and we all felt pretty bad for him.'

The other Liberator belonging to Lieutenant James was also forced to land in Turkey. Earl Zimmerman, the radio-operator recalls: 'We met the remainder of the Mooney crew—the wounded members having been immediately taken to hospital and later returned to the States. We stayed overnight at a rooming house and next day, 2 August, a funeral was held for Captain Mooney at a small cemetery outside Izmir. During the procession through the town, Mooney's coffin was taken by the front of the German Consulate despite German protests.

'The day after the funeral we were taken to the railway station for a nice long trip to Ankara. It was a real hairy trip—their trains at that time something to behold. But we arrived in the Turkish capital to be put up in the Turkish Military Academy which was on summer vacation at the time on the outskirts of the city. We were put on the third floor where we met five more crews but they were incomplete, some having been wounded and others missing. It got quite overcrowded and we counted, including ourselves, sixty-four people. We were met by General R. G. Tindall, Military Attaché at the American Embassy and members of his staff, including his assistant, Major Brown. We were now under their jurisdiction and we were to take orders from them. We were briefed and most of the internees were looking forward to some good food like ice-cream and nice fresh melons.

'Later the school restarted and we were moved to the Yeni (New) Hotel. On the night of 27 September sixteen British boys showed up at the Yeni. They did not give us too much information but I got the impression that they were flying some kind of secret mission, probably out of Cyprus into Greece or the Balkans and had got shot down off the coast of Turkey. Their escape procedures were so much better than ours. They were only in the Yeni Hotel two days and when we woke up one morning they were all gone! We asked the Turkish guards where they had gone but they said they didn't know!

'Our arrangements were that we would sign out on parole each day from 09.00 to 22.00 hours. We were given direct orders not to violate the parole period at any time—even when attempting to escape! Arrangements, however, were made with the Turkish Government. According to the Geneva Convention if one was ill one could sign off parole so some kind of deal was made so we were sick every day! No-one ever violated the parole and on some occasions we got special permission to stay out after parole if one of the embassies threw a party.

'But it got boring after a while and thoughts turned to escape. While at the Military Academy a mass break out was attempted. Seventeen managed to get out but two were caught near the Syrian border and returned. Although not a complete success it was well engineered. A fake brawl was started by about ten to fifteen American internees on the third floor and when the Turkish responded they were promptly pulled into the fray, their rifles being held by us, the bystanders! When it was determined that some of the doors were left unguarded everyone took off for the hills.'Earl Zimmerman followed his pilot, First Lieutenant Harold L. James, only to be caught and held as they reached an exit on the first floor.

Earl Zimmerman was a qualified radio man and for a time operated a radio sending reports to Washington via Cairo. His rig barely reached Cairo where the Signal Corps picked up his transmission but they could and did fire off messages to Washington at 150 wpm. Prior to Zimmerman's arrival in Turkey, messages took a long time reaching the ZI.

'It got to be a pretty routine thing every day in Ankara and every once in a while the Embassy would sneak a few of us out the back door to Africa and back to England. In December 1943 my chance finally came. By this time I was glad of the opportunity. Although we had a certain freedom we were not allowed to leave Ankara. On 16 December I signed the payroll at the embassy, packed my belongings and was one of those given orders to escape that day! The Germans at this time were kicking up a storm about all the escapes being made so the Turks had to tread pretty lightly. At night six of us, in ones and twos, left for the railway station. Just before the train pulled out for Syria we jumped on board. However, I noticed the senior Turkish officer in charge of internees simply salute as we left the station! We gratefully returned his salute. It was a pretty rough train ride. I slept on the baggage rack above the seats and the others slept on the floor and on the seats. The train pulled into Aleppo, Syria, where we were met by the British. We stayed there for a couple of days before a C-47 flew in and took us to Camp Huckstep in Cairo. We were in civilian clothing and under strict orders not to tell anyone where we were going or where we had come from.'

Most of Lieutenant James's crew returned to operations. Earl Zimmerman filling in as a spare radio man on some missions. But while he was grounded one day the gunners flew a mission and did not come back.

Of the 177 Liberators which took part in the Ploesti raid, fifty-four failed to return. The plants which they had sought to destroy were repaired and operating at pre-mission capacity within a month.

The Anvil Project

From the very outset of the war in Europe one of the Allies' greatest fears was Germany's top secret 'wonder weapons'. The first to emerge was the V1 'Flying Bomb' nicknamed the 'Doodlebug'. But to a certain extent this threat was contained by artillery chains on the south coast of England. High speed piston and later, jet aircraft also shot them down or skimmed their control surfaces, upsetting their sensitive gyroscopes and causing them to crash. But there was one 'wonder weapon' which could not be stopped by conventional means. The V2 rocket could travel faster than the speed of sound and penetrate targets from an altitude inaccessible to the aircraft of the day. 'Big Ben' jamming operations had proved unsuccessful so the only way to stop the V2s was to bomb their launching sites. This had already been tried by conventional bombers against the V1 sites but with limited success. It was not uncommon for B-17s and B-24s to make one, two and even as many as six bomb runs over the 'No Ball' sites, as they were known. Even so on the majority of occasions the sites remained intact.

The V2 sites called for something more than conventional bombing techniques. By the summer of 1944 revolutionary 'Azon' glider bombs had already been used against bridges in France. These devices were basically conventional 1000 lb bombs fitted with radio-controlled moveable tail fins. Visibility was all important to enable the radio operators in the Liberators, the aircraft used for the project, to keep a visual sighting on the glider bomb right up to the target. For this purpose each had a smoke canister attached. But the effectiveness of the 'stand off' bomb was limited and the project was subsequently abandoned in June 1944. At about this time General James Doolittle, the US Air Force Chief in the Pacific, revealed that his bombers too had tried bombing by means of radio-controlled glide bombs. Like the 'Azon' bombs his 160 knot 'Torpeckers' had met with little success. Seven glider bombs had been used against positions on the Japanese-held island of Truk in the Pacific and all had been destroyed at will by the Japanese defences. It was apparent that some other method would have to be found if the V2 sites were to be destroyed from the air.

The 'Azon' idea was taken one stage further and it was decided that the aircraft themselves would form the warhead. Like the glider bombs they would be directed to their target by radio. The United States Navy had been experimenting with remotely controlled 'drones' since 1937 but belief that there were four V2 sites in the Pas de Calais ready to rain rockets on London, gave the project a new sense of urgency. (By the middle of 1944 it was thought that Mimoyecques, Siracourt, Watten, and Wizernes were the most likely sites for the launching of the V2s). The United States Strategic Air Forces' response to meet the threat was quick and decisive.

Two parallel projects were put forward, 'Aphrodite' and 'Anvil', the one proposed by the Army Air Corps and the other by the US Navy. Both these projects called for bombers packed with high explosive to be flown by two-man crews who would bail out over England and the rest of the flight to be taken over by 'mother' aircraft whose operators would guide the 'drones' to their targets by remote control. The method chosen included a television camera installed in the nose of the drone and a receiver set in the controlling aircraft. This enabled the controllers to view the approach of the target as if they were in the nose of the drone itself. Controlling the drone and arming the explosives once the crew had baled out were effected by means of radio signals from the mother aircraft.

General Carl 'Tooey' Spaatz, Commanding Officer of the Eighth Air Force in England, at first proposed to General 'Hap' Arnold, Chief of Air Staff, that war weary fighters be used. But these were discarded in favour of bombers which could carry more high explosive. Forty unwanted B-17s were stripped, cannabilized, and fitted with crude radios. Seventeen pilots and crew volunteered from the bomber groups in England, a number which was increased later. The B-17s were at first based at Woodbridge in Suffolk but one night a Luftwaffe pilot, tried to make use of the base FIDO (Fog Indication and Dispersal Operation) apparatus. Because of the secrecy involved 'Project Aphrodite' was relocated lest the German pilot had radioed to Germany of the operation, at Fersfield in Suffolk. Fersfield was ideal because experiments on 'Batty' and 'Glomb', primitive radio-controlled glider bombs launched from aircraft, were already being tested there.

The 'Anvil' project arose from the

Lieutenant Joseph P. Kennedy Jnr. USNR. Photographed in 1943.

44

Azon Liberators of the 458th Group.

enthusiasm of Admiral King of the US Navy who placed the Navy's experience of radio-controlled drones at the Army's disposal. The US Navy did not possess Flying Fortresses so PB4Ys, the Naval version of the B-24 Liberator, were used. They had the advantage over the B-17s of being able to carry a bigger bomb load. The systems installed in the 'Aphrodite' Fortresses were to be installed in the PB4Ys which had spent many hours roaming over the freezing waters of the northern Atlantic on anti-submarine patrols.

In late July 1944 a Dakota carrying a group of high ranking Naval officers arrived at Dunkeswell air base in Devon from a highly secret airbase in Florida to co-ordinate the work which the Navy designated SAU-1 (Special Attack Unit). On board were Commander James A. Smith who was to command the project, and his executive officer, Lieutenant Wilford 'Bud' Willy, a pilot and a leading expert on radio control.

Volunteers were called upon to fly the lethal explosive-packed aircraft. They came from VB-110, the Navy squadron that used Dunkeswell. Among them was a twenty-nine year old pilot from Massachusetts with a famous name and an equally famous past. He was Lieutenant Joe Kennedy Junior, son of the former United States' Ambassador to Britain, Joseph P. Kennedy. Joe Junior's brother John (later to become President of the United States) also served in the Navy, as a commander of an MTB in the Pacific.

Joe Kennedy Junior had attended Harvard University before the war and from 1938 to 1939 had served consecutively as a Private Secretary in the American embassies in London and Paris. He returned to Harvard in 1939 and attended Law School until October 1941 when he was appointed an Aviation cadet in the US Naval Reserve. On 16 October he reported to Jacksonville, Florida for flight training and by April 1942 had risen to Ensign. After a further eight months' duty with a transition training squadron Joe Kennedy joined a patrol squadron in 1943 and advanced to Lieutenant Junior

Grade in May that year. In July 1943 he was transferred to the US Navy's VB-110 Squadron.

By the summer of 1944 Joe Junior had completed his tour of operations without gaining a combat medal. He reasoned that D-Day would either be in June or July and did not intend missing out on the action. Having just completed thirty-five missions he volunteered for another tour. But D-Day came and went and Lieutenant Kennedy had still not claimed an enemy craft. He became less cautious and even more determined in his pursuit of a submarine or E-boat. On 1 July 1944 Joe Kennedy was promoted to Lieutenant and was soon offered the post of Assistant Naval Attaché at the US Embassy in London. But he refused as he was as determined as ever to carve his niche in naval aviation. His chance came when Commander Smith asked for volunteers to fly the 'flying bombs' against German targets. Joe had no hesitation in putting his name forward and despite attempts by his Commanding Officer, Commander Reedy, to talk him out of it, the young Kennedy got his wish. He and Dee Vilan, a radio operator, and Bradfield, a pilot, were posted to SAU-1.

In early July 1944 the first 'Anvil' Liberator was modified as a drone at the Naval Air Material Centre in Philadelphia. A control system and an arming panel were installed. Meanwhile, two Lockheed PV1 Venturas were flown to Philadelphia and modified as 'mother' aircraft to the Liberator. A week's crash course followed and finished with mother, child, and the men of 'Project Anvil' setting off across the Atlantic for Dunkeswell. For seven days the PB4Y was prepared for its sacrificial mission. All non-essential equipment like the co-pilot's seat and the bomb-bay racks were removed. The aircraft was completely gutted and new supports were installed to shore up the fuselage to take the additional weight. Normally a B-24 Liberator would carry a bomb load of 5,000 lb on long and 8,000 lb on short-range raids. But the 'Anvil' PB4Ys were required to carry twelve crates of Torpex; twelve times the load of a V1.

Security at Dunkeswell was extremely tight and all personnel were sworn to secrecy. In fact the project was so secret that when the machine-guns were removed from the Liberators they were replaced with black-painted broomsticks in case the Luftwaffe flew over and took a glance. Mechanics toiled on the bombers for hours at a stretch removing oxygen tanks, antenna, and radarscopes. Oak-frame cradles replaced the bomb-racks because the weight of the explosive had to be spread throughout the entire fuselage. This meant that on the actual flight the two-man crew would have to bale out through the nose-wheel hatch, the rear hatch being blocked with explosives. For easier identification the Liberator's olive drab wings and fuselage were whitewashed over and a beacon was fixed to the tail fin. Baffles were fitted immediately in front of the nose-wheel

doors to deflect the slipstream away from the crew when they bailed out. Inside, a radar beacon was installed which enabled the controller in the 'mother' ship to obtain a 'fix' on the drone.

After a week of preparations Joe Kennedy's chance came to fly the drone. On 30 July 1944 he took Vilan and Bradfield on a thirty-minute test flight. The PBY4, relieved of all its armament and not yet carrying its lethal cargo, took off from Dunkeswell effortlessly. Checks were carried out in flight but no problems were encountered. Commander Smith was satisfied that 'Anvil' was ready and movement to Fersfield began at once. Later that day Kennedy piloted the drone to the Suffolk base. As he flew in he could see the 'Aphrodite' Fortresses dispersed inside the base perimeter which had been sealed off from the public. Over 2,000 men from the Eighth Air Force and the RAF had been gather at Fersfield and security was tight. Even today locals insist that when missions began smoke-screens were laid at the beginning of each flight. Guard dogs, too, patrolled the perimeter. The Naval complement of twenty officers and sixteen crewmen lost no time settling into their new accommodation. The Quonset huts with their soft mattresses were a welcome change from the huts at 'Mudville Heights' at Dunkeswell.

'Aphrodite' and 'Anvil' personnel began to work in harmony under the over-all control of the Eighth Air Force Third Bombardment Division which had its headquarters at Elveden Hall, near Thetford, Norfolk. Logistic support was provided by the 388th Bombardment Group which was flying Fortress bombing missions from near-by Knettishall.

At first a special radio search of the air waves was made to make sure that the enemy was not using frequencies on which it was proposed to operate the drones. Then test flights with simulated loads were made. These were achieved by stowing sacks containing 15,000 lb of sand inside the Liberator. Joe Kennedy made the first test flight on 2 August with Lieutenant John Anderson at the controls of the Ventura 'mother' ship. Joe had great difficulty taking off and the landing, too, proved awkward with the simulated cargo. But Kennedy and Anderson practised the remote control procedure until Joe became accustomed to the shaky handling characteristics. All that was required now was a period of suitably fine weather.

Two days later the Fersfield base commander, Lieutenant Colonel Roy Forrest, ordered four 'Aphrodite' B-17s to bomb a V1 site. P-38 fighter escorts and Liberator 'mother' ships joined the entourage, which headed for a 'No-Ball' site in the Pas de Calais. Each B-17 carried ten tons of RDX, not as lethal or as big a load as the Liberators could carry, but enough to create a sizeable crater. Unlike the PB4Y the RDX arming procedure was completed manually.

But none of the B-17s reached their intended targets. Two were shot down and the other two crashed and exploded, one after the crew had bailed out. On 6 August two more drones left Fersfield. One crashed into the Channel and the other exploded just after the crew bailed out over East Anglia.

Despite these misfortunes the Navy decided to go ahead with their 'Anvil' drone. The weather forecast was good and so on 11 August 1944, 21,170 lbs of Torpex was distributed throughout the Liberator together with six demolition charges each containing 113 lb of TNT. A twenty-four-hour guard was placed while the loading of the 374 crates commenced. There were 17 crates on the flight-deck, 16 in the nose-wheel compartment, 313 in the bomb-bays and 28 on the command deck. All were kept in place by four inch square pine timbers and secured to the bulkhead and main supports by quarter inch steel cable. Frequent checks were maintained during loading for possible static electrical charging that could detonate the load. By 12.00 hours Tom Martin, the ordnance expert, declared the Liberator ready.

This mission was cancelled because of fog although it had almost ended altogether when one of the men loading the Liberator dropped a crate of Torpex five feet to the ground.

Joe Kennedy was chosen to fly the Navy's first mission, now scheduled for 12 August. The target selected being the secret weapon site at Mimoyecques. At that time, unknown to the Allies, it actually concealed a three-barrelled 150 mm artillery piece, designed to fire 600 tons of explosive a day on London. The Navy had already insisted on additional safety measures that had not been carried on the earlier B-17 attempts. The arming device on board the Liberator had a metal pin inserted in a plywood panel behind the pilot to prevent vibration prematurely cocking the arming solenoid. It would also prevent static electricity or radio signals setting it off accidentally as had happened in America. A rip cord was attached to the pin and Joe was to pull the handle on the end of the rip cord, thus releasing the safety

Officers of US Navy Squadron VB-110 at Dunkeswell, Devon, 10 March 1944 in front of one of the Squadron's PB4Y-1 Liberators. Joseph Kennedy is back row, far left. In the front row right, is John Kellogg who flew with Kennedy.

pin, before bailing out.

'Bud' Willy was selected as Kennedy's co-pilot. Despite protestations from some quarters they decided they would not bail out until they had reached Dover. This was in complete contrast to the B-17 crews who always bailed out ten minutes after take-off. However, Willy and Kennedy wanted to be sure that the drone would remain in human hands until it had passed London, fifty miles to starboard on the flight path. It would also allow Anderson ample time to obtain full control of the drone. As a further safety precaution it was decided that two Venturas would accompany the drone in case one became unserviceable in flight. The bale-out point for Kennedy and Willy would be near RAF Manston. Between Clacton-on-Sea and Manston the co-pilot would check the arming circuit with a safety-lamp. Only if the circuit was safe would the safety pin be removed and the connection made to the firing solenoid to permit Anderson's operator to carry out the remote arming.

The plan called for 'Bud' Willy to bale out through the nose-wheel doors followed by Kennedy, who would first pull a set of manual arming toggles for the contact fuses. Both men were issued with rescue parachutes and a double-length static line to reduce the shock of the parachute opening. A B-17 was to navigate for the mission and after Kennedy and Willy had bailed out would monitor their descent so that they could be picked up and returned to Fersfield. The 'drone' would be remotely armed for detonation on impact only after it had left the English coast.

Fersfield was vibrant with the knowledge that the Navy were to fly their first 'Anvil' mission. At the briefing Kennedy and Willy learned that their Liberator would be code-named 'Zootsuit Black' and the two Venturas, 'Zootsuit Pink' and 'Zootsuit Red'. At 14.00 hours it was announced that the mission would definitely go ahead and three hours later Commander Smith and Lieutenant-Colonel Forrest returned to Fersfield in a droop snoot P-38J bearing favourable weather reports for the Channel and target area.

At 17.52 hours the two Venturas took off from Fersfield right on schedule and circled the airfield. Kennedy's aircraft had had magneto trouble in number three engine right up to the start of the mission and at take-off time Joe ran all the engines for a few minutes to make certain they were running smoothly. He seemed satisfied and released the Liberator's brakes. It staggered along the runway and shortly afterwards a Mustang, a P-38 Lightning flown by Lieutenant-Colonel Cass Hough, and two weather reconnaissance Mosquitoes which filmed the take-off, followed in the Liberator's wake. High over Suffolk flew sixteen Mustang escorts.

The formation continued at 2,000 feet to Framlingham where they were to change course for Beccles. At 18.15 hours, just before Framlingham was reached, Kennedy radioed that he was ready for the first Ventura to carry out the first radio control check. This involved turning the Liberator left over Framlingham by remote control and on to its new course for Beccles. This manoeuvre was successfully completed. The second stage of the mission was proceeding satisfactorily when suddenly the drone was ripped apart by two explosions over Saxmundham at 1,500 feet. The turbulence tossed the trailing aircraft all over the sky and one Mosquito on its back. The other Mosquito, flown by Lieutenants Tunnell and McCarthy, was damaged by the blast, as McCarthy recalls:

'We had just decided to close in on the baby. I was flying in the nose of the plane so that I could get some good shots of the Baby in flight ahead of us. The Baby just exploded in mid-air. As we heard it I was knocked half way back to the cockpit. A few pieces of the Baby came through the plexiglass nose and I got hit in the head and caught a lot of fragments in my right arm. I crawled back to the cockpit and lowered the wheels so that Bob could make a quick emergency landing.'

A hail of wreckage spread over the countryside. In the radius of half a mile over 150 houses were damaged. A Lightning spun away to port and only managed to regain control at tree-top height. One Ventura broke high to starboard. For many minutes the stunned crews circled the burning wreckage which had fallen over a wide area around Newdelight Covert between Dunwich and Blythburgh but there was nothing they could do and they returned, shaken, to Fersfield.

Back at Fersfield, eighteen miles distant, operators had witnessed the monitor screen suddenly 'snow' and go blank. At the same time a slight tremor was felt in the hut. When the Ventura pilots confirmed their worst fears the men at Fersfield were desolate and some close to tears. The search for the cause of the explosion began immediately and at first suspicion was cast on the remote arming switches in the Venturas. They were examined as soon as the two-engined aircraft landed but they were still wired in their 'safe' positions. Rumours of sabotage or enemy jamming were rife and the crews were interrogated at the debriefing. But they were adamant that the arming circuit switches had remained untouched. One by one the possibilities were ruled out. Sabotage was discounted because of the tight security screen and the guards had reported nothing unusual. Static electricity, too, was believed not to have been the cause. The Liberator been carefully earthed and the air during the flight was smooth. The possibility that Torpex was to blame was eliminated as it had no reputation for instability. Even fuel leaks which might have been ignited by a spark were discounted because there had been no history of such leaks.

Another proposal put forward strongly at the time was the possibility that there had been interference from frequencies used by the RAF's 'Big Ben' sets in use for jamming V2 signals. But the relevant observation of the cause of the disaster came from an onlooker who, just before the explosion, saw a thin trail of black smoke which seemed to emanate from the rear weapon bay. It would seem then that there was overheating in the electrical circuitry of the arming panel and later tests indicated weaknesses in the hastily assembled and installed remote arming and fusing arrangements.

A report on the crash was prepared and one of its recommendations was that a second PBY4 drone be readied with utmost dispatch for employment against the enemy at the earliest possible moment. But by the time it was ready to fly against an enemy target the Saint-Lô breakthrough had occurred and the Allied ground forces had captured the Normandy rocket-launching sites. It was decided, therefore, that the second Navy drone should be flown against submarine pens on the island of Heligoland. The mission took place on 3 September 1944 and British stations jamming V2 signals were ordered to stand down that day. Lieutenant Ralph D. Spalding successfully took off from Fersfield and baled out through the nose-wheel hatch after manually arming the drone. It was then guided to Heligoland by a 'mother' ship but missed the submarine pens. For his efforts Spalding was awarded the Navy Cross. He was killed on 14 January 1945 in an air crash in North Africa on his way back to the United States.

Spalding's mission was the last the Navy flew. The Air Force continued operations until New Year's Day 1944 but of the seventeen Air Force missions and two Navy missions, none of the drones hit the target. Allied advances in France soon overran the secret weapon sites and the RAF possessed the capability to destroy targets of this nature with their 'Grand Slam' earthquake bombs anyway.

Because of the secrecy attached to the project and probably because the Allied authorities did not want to alarm the population over whose countryside these lethal bombers flew, Kennedy's crash was kept secret. The authorities even went so far at the time as to move the scene of the crash. Many war correspondents knew either part or all of the story but were bound to secrecy and it was not until 24 October 1945 that the full story was released to the Press and radio. Although the projects did not achieve wartime success post-war adaptations succeeded in creating a 'ghost' Hellcat which by means of radio could fly by itself.

The bravery of Lieutenant Kennedy and Lieutenant Willy and that of all the 'Aphrodite' and 'Anvil' volunteer crews deserves the highest praise. Kennedy and Willy were both decorated and Joe's father, Joseph S. Kennedy Senior, received the Navy Cross on his son's behalf.

The citation read:

'For extraordinary heroism and courage in aerial flight as a pilot of a United States Navy Liberator bomber on August 12, 1944. Well knowing the extreme dangers involved and totally unconcerned for his own safety, Lieutenant Kennedy unhesitatingly volunteered to conduct an exceptionally hazardous and special operational mission. Intrepid and daring in his tactics and with unwavering confidence in the vital performance of his task, he willingly risked his life in the supreme measure of service and, by his great personal valor and fortitude in carrying out a perilous undertaking, sustained and enhanced the finest traditions of the United States Naval Service.'

Joseph P. Kennedy poses in light-hearted mood at Dunkeswell.

Below: *A 458th crew chief gives the signal to cut engines to a B-24 at Horsham St Faith.*

Inset Left: *One of two B-24As which took some of the Harriman mission to Moscow, via England, in September 1941. The stars and stripes are prominently displayed to proclaim American neutrality.*

Inset Right: *A Liberator of the Return Ferry Service passes over Montreal shortly before landing.*

Cheek to Cheek, Nose to Tail

The B-24 Liberator was one of the most maligned aircraft of the Second World War. It was lampooned by cartoonists and B-24 aircrews alike. Much of the derision originated from the Liberator's shape. A long graceful high-aspect ratio wing was offset by a vast billboard styled body but it served as a perfect canvas for Air Force artists and cartoonists the world over.

Much of the inspiration came from loved ones at home, in the form of shapely figures on the noses of their Liberators. Like figure-heads on ships they rode through the extremes of the Atlantic to England across the dusty deserts of North Africa to Italy. Some carried their sweethearts' names beneath the art work while others made their intentions clear to the enemy with taunts of *Flak Dodger* and *Hitler's Hearse.* They epitomized the spirit of these young aircrews, their exuberance sometimes landing them in trouble with those in authority. Almost all Liberator nose art, and for that matter, B-17 too, centred on the nude female form. Headquarters initiated, without success, a short-lived campaign to 'clean-up' the art work of some of the more revealing models. Their creators responded with skimpy briefs and negligées which made their models look even more alluring.

Two of the greatest influences upon the abundance of work to be found on the noses of aircraft were the Li'l Abner comic strip characters created by the legendary Al Capp and the superb Alberto Vargas female creations which appeared in the magazine *Esquire.* Al Capp had begun his salty satirical strip in the Depression year of 1934. The hill-billy village of Dogpatch, which satirized Washington and its Presidents from Franklin D. Roosevelt onwards, introduced Abner Yokum, the innocent country boy and his community of rural loafers and greedy politicians. At its peak the cartoon strip featured in 900 newspapers and many Britons first introduction came from the comic sections of American newspapers which were wrapped round post-war food parcels. However, every day, for miles around each air base gum-chewing British children were able to see Al Capp's characters almost life-size on the noses of the aircraft. Apart from Li'l Abner, which graced many a bomber there was Abner's repulsive mother, the pipe-smoking Mammy Yokum and Daisy Mae Scragg, a blonde whose clothes became more tattered and revealing as she strove to win the heart of the insensitive Li'l Abner. There was also Marryin' Sam the marriage broker, Hairless Joe, the maker of Kickapoo Joy Juice and Lena the

Hyena, the ugliest woman in the world, which came as a shock to B-17 crews who thought the B-24 was.

The superlative Vargas watercolours had appeared well before the catastrophe of Pearl Harbor on the covers of *Esquire*. As the war heightened this magazine's unabashed patriotism and militarism led the field with the Peruvian artist's scantily-clad females in the forefront. The 'Varga' girl became the symbol of the serviceman's dreams and he decorated his barracks with the calendars and played cards with decks emblazoned with them. Then he painted his aircraft. In the summer of 1943 Vargas was signed up by *American Weekly* for a series of twelve paintings aimed at specific branches of the military services. Late in 1944 he agreed to paint a new and different 'Varga' girl for the back covers of the military edition of the magazine. And so the pin-up was well and truly launched, not only in the magazines but also on the aluminium-stressed skin of the bombers of all the air forces throughout the world.

'Miss December' 1944 became *Wistful Vista* of the 446th Bomber Group in England while the *Esquire* gatefold 'There'll Always Be a Christmas', of 1943 enhanced *Heavenly Body*. Other gatefolds like 'Patriotic Gal', 'Warning Signal', 'Military Secrets' appealed to the serviceman and the June 1944 gatefold 'Matrimony Preferred' was most appropriate for loved ones far away. The 'Varga' girls appeared throughout the war and became a symbol of the American fighting man.

Walt Disney's Mickey Mouse (which also lent its name to the 'Mickey' radar bombing aid) and Donald Duck, and Warner Brothers' 'Bugs Bunny' also appeared on bombers. But others were unique creations of single Liberator groups and squadrons. In the early years of the

war the 44th Bomber Group, soon to join the 2nd Bomb Division of the Eighth Air Force in England, called themselves the 'Eightballs' after the black ball in the game of Pool. The 44th was broken up to form other groups and those personnel that remained called themselves the 'Eightballs'. A distinctive emblem was designed and in the summer of 1942 was painted on the nose of each of the Group's B-24Ds. When the 44th began flying to England in late 1942 the Group became known as 'The Flying Eightballs' and each aircraft sported a black eightball with a nose, wings, and a bomb for a body.

In North Africa and Italy the 343rd Bomber Squadron of Colonel 'Killer' Kane's 98th Bomber Group was unique in that all the Liberators were decked out with characters from Walt Disney's cartoon film *Snow White and the Seven Dwarfs*. Kane's 'Pyramiders' flew to Ploesti with *Grumpy* renamed *Hail Columbia* especially for the big occasion. *Snow White* herself was the 'flagship' for the squadron.

In the Far East and Pacific theatres could be found some of the most impressive designs of all. The 43rd Bomb Squadron on Ie Shima boasted some of the very best, literally from nose to tail on their Liberators at the end of the war. *The Dragon and His Tail* stretched from the nose to the tail while *It Ain't So Funny* featured almost every cartoon character from Popeye to Batman while the 486th Bomber Group liberally sprinkled the signs of the Zodiac on the noses of their Liberators.

In sharp contrast, US Navy Liberators were less lavish and more 'down to earth'. Paul Stevens of the 'Buccaneers' of VPB 104 in the Pacific recalls that their aircraft had little in the way of decoration. Even bomb symbols were not allowed. This was all part of the US Navy's 'professional' approach to air operations and crews preferred not to tip the Japanese off

Extreme Left: The Li'l Abner comic strip cartoon lent itself to many examples of nose art. Featured here are Hairless Joe of the 493rd BG (8th AF), Pappy's Yokum of the 491st and later the 467th, Daisy Mae Scraggs and Sweet Moonbeam McSwine both from the 446th, Dogpatch Express of the 459th (15th AF) and of course Li'l Abner pictured in the North African desert in 1942.

Left: Cocktail Hour of the 43rd at Ie Shima in late 1945.

Centre Top: The Dragon and his Tail also of the 43rd at Ie Shima.

Centre Bottom: An original piece of graphics on Booby Trap.

Right Top: Snow White and the Seven Dwarfs from the 343rd Bomber Squadron all of whose aircraft depicted characters from this film.

Right Centre: Plutocrat from the 458th based at Horsham St Faith, England.

Right Bottom: Walt Disney characters featured largely on USAAF Liberators but RAF crews also used them particularly in the Far East, where there was a strong Canadian influence. Donald Duck is seen here featured on a Liberator belonging to 159 Squadron at Salbani, India.

Top: *At the end of the Pacific war some beautiful murals appeared on Liberators of the 43rd BG such as* Mabel's Labels *at Ie Shima.*

Below: The Goon, *a Liberator from the 308th BG, 14th Airforce, the only B-24 group to operate from China.*

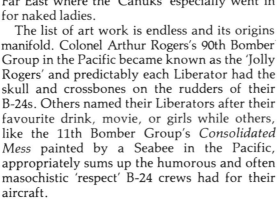

about how many missions they had flown if they were unfortunate enough to be shot down and captured.

However, Commander Harry Sears, of VPB 104 christened his second aircraft *Mark's Farts* while his successor, Lieutenant-Commander Whitney Wright, felt obliged to use a Liberator called *Whitsshits*. Equally earthy were the RAF and TCAF decorations on their Liberators in the Far East where the 'Canuks' especially went in for naked ladies.

The list of art work is endless and its origins manifold. Colonel Arthur Rogers's 90th Bomber Group in the Pacific became known as the 'Jolly Rogers' and predictably each Liberator had the skull and crossbones on the rudders of their B-24s. Others named their Liberators after their favourite drink, movie, or girls while others, like the 11th Bomber Group's *Consolidated Mess* painted by a Seabee in the Pacific, appropriately sums up the humorous and often masochistic 'respect' B-24 crews had for their aircraft.

Above: *The skull and crossbones on a Liberator of Colonel Arthur Roger's 90th BG—'The Jolly Rogers'.*

Right: *The alluring nose art of* Kentucky Belle *from the 446th BG, 2nd AD, Bungay, England.*

Extreme Right: Shoo, Shoo, Baby *inspired by 'Torches at Midnight' the Vargas pin-up of 1943.*

Left: A 458th crew wait by their Liberator Arise My Lovely And Come With Me, *prior to a mission. The model has been partly obscured by armour plating, fitted for the pilot's protection.*

Below: Ground staff painting bombs beneath the tail of a Liberator of the 451st BG, 15th AF.

Extreme Left: Lady Luck of the 446th, thought to be one of 'Rosie's Riveters', the factory girls who helped make the Liberators. The design was featured on many B-24s.

Left: Un-named nose art depicting Donald Duck on a B-24J of the 446th at Bungay, England.

55

Pathfinders

One of the early problems for aircrews during the Second World War was the finding and bombing of targets in cloudy conditions. The Americans discovered that overcast conditions seemed to predominate not only over their British bases during assembly but also over their European targets. Daylight missions were fraught with collisions, which were only partly alleviated by the use of assembly ships. Even more worrying was their lack of success in finding overcast targets and hitting them.

It was the British who overcame the problem of navigation and bombing in cloudy conditions using the 'Gee' navigational device. 'Gee' was first used by RAF Bomber Command aircraft in 1941. Sets in the aircraft received pulse transmissions from ground stations made up of one master and two slave transmitters. Differences in the arrival of signals from these three points enabled the navigator to 'fix' the position of his aircraft by referring to two 'Gee' co-ordinates. These were printed as a grid on special 'Gee' charts ('Gee' derives from 'G' for Grid).

Late in 1942, Eighth Air Force Liberators from the 93rd Bomb Group experimented with 'Gee' on daylight 'Moling' or 'Intruder' flights over Germany which were an attempt to disrupt working schedules in German factories by causing air raid sirens to sound, upsetting civilian morale, and impairing industrial output. These B-24s operated singly because of the experimental nature of the work and the cloudy conditions provided their only defence. The 'Moling' project was abandoned in March 1943 but it was instrumental in providing the Pathfinders with a nucleus of crews experienced in blind bombing techniques.

Two other precision radio-radar bombing aids were developed by the British—H2S and 'Oboe'. H2S was an airborne radar scanner which displayed a rough outline of the terrain below on a cathode ray tube. It had earned its name from remarks made by Professor Lindemann, one of Winston Churchill's chief advisers, who said it was 'stinking' that it had not been invented sooner. (H2S, Hydrogen Sulphide, smells like rotten eggs.) 'Oboe' was a very accurate bombing aid which actually allowed bombs (or markers) to be dropped by the ground controller. This was achieved by the aircraft retransmitting signals received from a master station (Cat). The master station controller measured the time delay and triggered off a slave station (Mouse) about 140 miles away. The 'Mouse' signal was received by

Left: A Liberator of the 392nd BG flies through heavy flak above totally overcast conditions. France, 10 August 1943.

Right: *A PFF ship of the 392nd leads the raid to the Braunkhale Synthetic Oil Works on 3 March 1945. Note the additional window amidships for the Radio Operator who vacated his seat on the flight deck for the Radar Operator.*

the aircraft and this in turn was retransmitted by the aircraft to the 'Cat' station. The controller could thereby determine the aircraft's exact location. A joke among navigators was whether to drop their bombs 'on number nine Wilhelmstrasse or number eleven'—it was that accurate.

The installation and operation of such devices made it prudent for a special USAAF group to be set up and in August 1943 the 482nd (Pathfinder) Group was formed at Alconbury. This group, the first and only American heavy bomber group to be formed on English soil, was equipped with one Liberator squadron and two B-17 squadrons. Their task was threefold. Apart from combat missions, and developing and testing radar devices, the 482nd was also charged with the training of Pathfinder crews. Primarily their task in the early months was to drop British smoke marker bombs guided by H2S to pinpoint the release point for the following formations.

In January 1944 the first factory-built American AN/APS-15 (H2X) 'Mickey' sets began to arrive, replacing the virtually homemade radar sets. With a supply of equipment assured, the Eighth Air Force decided upon a policy of dispersion for its 'Pathfinders'. New crews were to be trained in 482nd methods and other 'Pathfinder' organizations were to be set up in the three Air Divisions. The 482nd was chosen to train them and they went to work with vigour.

On 11 January 1944 the Eighth Air Force decided to attack five aircraft plants in the Brunswick area. The mission was memorable as it was the first time the 482nd provided Liberators as 'Pathfinders'. The weather deteriorated during the first two hours of the mission and an abnormally high cloud began to close in over the target areas effectively reducing and splitting the escorting fighters. Command was forced to recall the Second and Third Air Divisions together with PFF Liberators but the First Air Division continued to Oschersleben with disastrous results. Among the 34 Fortresses lost on the mission was an H2S 'Pathfinder'.

The second phase of the 482nd's history was radar research and development and training in the new techniques. The result was H2X Synchronous Bombing, a technique which enabled heavy bombers, led by crews of the 482nd Bomb Group, to pound German defences on the Normandy beaches on D-Day. Their accuracy was such that assault troops 1,000 yards offshore and isolated Paratroop units 800 yards inland manoeuvred in no danger from the great masses of bombs dropped on the narrow strip between. In support of the invasion, the 482nd Bomb Group flew twenty-four sorties, leading elements of the First and Third Bomb Divisions.

While all this research and development was going on, training was not permitted to lag. Over 1,100 navigators were trained in H2X and AN/APQ-7 for the Eighth and Fifteenth Air Forces and 2,000 radar mechanics were trained for work on H2X and AN/APQ-7 sets as well as 'Rebecca' (SCR-729), AN/APS-13, Gee, Gee-H, Loran, and RCM. When the V-bombs menaced England, specially trained Radar operator-mechanic photographers were sent by the Group to Hastings and Greyfriars. They produced continuous Scope motion picture records of the V-bomb's take-off and flight and alerted Fighter and Anti-Aircraft defences. This idea worked so well that soon 80 per cent of all V-bombs sent over were destroyed before landfall.

Two PFF ships lead in the 489th on a raid to the enemy installations at Hamburg and Harburg on 6 October 1944.

Assembly

Liberators formate on the 458th assembly ship Spotted Ape, *shortly after take-off from Horsham St Faith, England.*

Right Top: *A close-up of* Spotted Ape.

Right Centre: *A rare colour photograph of 466th's assembly ship at Attlebridge, England.*

Right Bottom: *The 467th assembly ship* Pete the POM Inspector. *Painted black overall with yellow discs outlined in red.*

The unusual concentration of bomber bases in East Anglia, and their proximity, demanded inviolate adherence to assembly procedure. Otherwise fatal accidents would result.

Aircraft were required to take-off 30 to 45 seconds apart, sometimes in zero ceiling with less than 500 yards visibility. Pilots knew beforehand the exact headings, speed, and distances separating each plane, and the length of each leg in the pattern they were to fly. For self-protection, all climbed at the same rate to the briefed spot where the assembly pattern took shape. And each group had its own buncher or splasher beacon for control points.

In this fashion they would sometimes climb through as much as 20,000 feet of overcast (80 to 90 minutes of instrument flying) in order to form on top, since assembly had to be made under conditions assuring 1,500 feet of clear air vertically.

Close knit formations were vital if high concentration of bomb impacts and effective mutual defence were to be achieved.

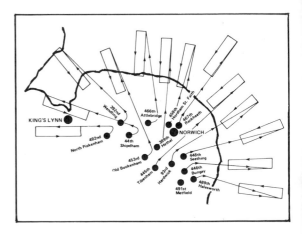

Gaudily painted assembly ships or 'Judas Goats'—war weary Liberators, stripped of all armament—shepherded their flock until the Group successfully formed up on their tails. Monitor ships—normally P-47 Thunderbolts flown by high ranking officers—were also employed to 'ride herd' on the formation, using radio commentary instead of flares.

Maintenance

Above: *Ground crew carrying out an engine change on a 15th AF Liberator at Brindisi in September 1943.*

Right: *Ground crews had to endure all kinds of conditions in all kinds of terrain.*

Top Left: *The 3rd SAD at Watton, Norfolk carried out thousands of repairs on 2nd AD Liberators. The most unusual must have been the temporary installation of a telegraph pole in the bomb-bay of* Pregnant Peg *to enable a recovery crew to fly it to Watton for repair.*

Top Right: Pregnant Peg *undergoing repairs in a 3rd SAD workshop at Watton.*

Centre: *Liberators undergoing repairs at BAD-2, Warton, Lancashire.*

Left: *RAF ground crew toil in the hot Indian sun during a propeller change on a 159 Squadron Liberator at Salbani.*

A formation of 93rd BG, B-24Ds based at Hardwick, England. Joisey Bounce is a veteran of Ploesti.

B-24Ds on the line at Wendover Field, Utah, behind them are the salt flats.

Two PFF B-24Js of the 93rd BG based at Hardwick, England en-route to their target.

Death and Destruction

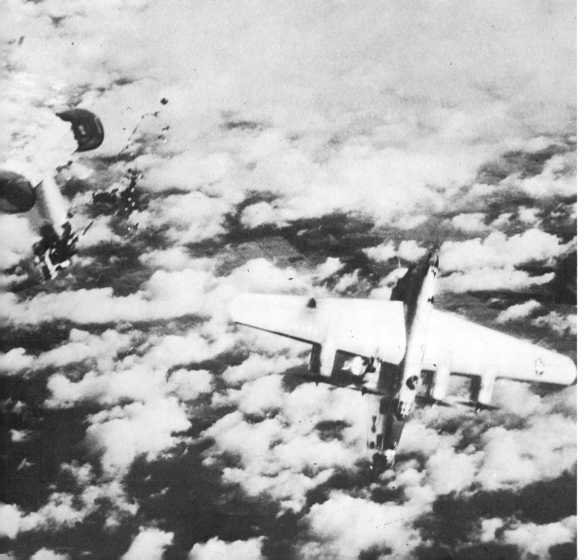

Extricating a wounded gunner from Liberty Lib of the 752nd BS, 458th BG, at Horsham St Faith, England.

A Liberator possibly from the 448th BG plummets to earth minus its tail section during a raid on the U-boat pens at Kiel and Hamburg.

Inset Top Left: Black Nan *a 'Micky' ship belonging to the 464th BG was hit by 88 mm flak during a mission on 9 April 1945. Lieutenant E. F. Walsh was the only survivor.*

Inset Top Centre: *An unidentified Liberator erupts into flames after receiving a direct hit in the fuel tanks.*

Inset Right Top: Little Warrior *of the 493rd BG begins to flame after receiving a direct flak hit during a raid on 29 June 1944 to Quakenbruk, Germany.*

Inset Right, Bottom Left: *A 389th BG Liberator begins to disintegrate as a result of enemy action.*

Inset Right, Bottom Right: *The Liberator minus a burning wing was all too common*

An ME109 turns away after successfully downing a Liberator.

Inset Left: *The grim reality of mid-air collision. The body of an 8th AF crew-member lies in an English field.*

Inset Right: *This B-24J piloted by Lieutenant Keith L. Frost of the 445th BG was hit over Coblenz during a raid on the marshalling yards on 10 November 1944 and flown back to Tibenham where it crash landed.*

Hotel Sweden
Frank Thomas

The Eighth Air Force often struck at the oil refineries on the Baltic and industrial conurbations on the Silesian Plain. If their bombers were too badly damaged to return over the North Sea B-24 and B-17 crews alike made for Sweden. One such crew which got into difficulties flew a 453rd Liberator based at Old Buckenham, Norfolk, England with the Second Bombardment Division of the Eighth Air Force. This crew, led by Kaylor C. Whitehead, had already experienced a forced landing in France in the autumn of 1944. Frank Thomas, the crew's radio-operator, recalls: 'We were flying our assigned ship, *Never Mrs*. Our main gasoline lines, hydraulic and electrical systems had been shot out. We had to land in France because we did not have enough fuel to make it back to England.

'We made for Vitry which we had actually bombed two weeks earlier but which had since fallen into Allied hands. In consequence we had to land on dirt, as the RAF Typhoons were doing. The RAF Wing Commander was typical of the cool efficient personnel we met during the next three days. Whitehead told him we would taxi to the hangar area, in order to be out of the way of his Typhoons. He answered, "Oh, I wouldn't do that, the Germans still hold that part of the area!"

'The Wing Commander assigned two welders to work with us. These two men worked wonders with what small pieces of fuel and hydraulic lines we were able to scrounge from the French countryside. The repairs completed and enough fuel for the flight back to England and Old Buckenham we planned our departure. I believe fifty per cent of the residents of the area gathered to see us attempt to take a B-24 out with only 3,800 feet of dirt before us. We made it, but the crowd sure had to scatter to give us that last few feet.

'It was on our return to the 453rd that we were given our nickname. We were surprised to find a huge banner on our 734th squadron barracks inscribed with the following message "Welcome Home—Whitehead's Tourist". The name stuck and our reputation of an almost uncanny luck grew.

'Our first visit to Hamburg, Germany, came on 30 October 1944. We found that area of Germany blanketed with a fog so thick and deep the mission was scrubbed—just as the bomb run should have begun. The absence of a PFF ship made it impossible to locate the target and complete the run. Everyone aborted except the "Tourist". We had no choice really. All our controls had iced up and the *Never Mrs* continued on her journey over Hamburg. We

Below: *Only two B-24s from the 466th landed in Sweden during the War. This is one of them* Lovely Lady's Avenger, *which crashed at Bulltofta on 21 June 1944. It was later scrapped.*

Centre: *Three B-24s and a B-17 parked at Västeras prior to being flown back to England. Left to right:* Hoo Jive, Salvaged Sally *and B-24 of the 389th.*

were in no way sure of the manoeuvres performed by her, until her wild gyrations and vibrations caused the ice to lose its grip on control cables and surfaces. We joined another B-24 group in the Cuxhaven area and returned to England. There we were accused of going on another sight-seeing tourist excursion!

'The stage for my second and third visits to Hamburg had been set. On my second scheduled visit to Hamburg I was called out to fly with another crew. Luckily, the mission was scrubbed but by this time the entire crew had developed a thing about Hamburg. The final omen was the loss of *Never Mrs* on 11 November 1944. She exploded over the Ruhr Valley on her seventieth mission—still running on the four original engines. She was carrying a new crew on their first mission and there were only four survivors. Your plane became almost as much a part of your life as did the men you flew with. Of course, the human life remained more important than the machine.

'We were awakened on the morning of 21 November, 1944 and informed the "Tourist" would fly today. Breakfast at the usual 12.30-1.00 a.m., briefing at 3.30 a.m. and take-off at 5.45 a.m. The same breakfast we had eaten so many times before—the trip to the line and the briefing room. Target: Hamburg-Harburg oil storage. Command Pilot (lead plane) was Colonel Van D. Dowda, his right wing plane (deputy lead), Captain E. E. Traylor's crew. (Traylor was a schoolmate of mine.) I believe Lieutenant Rollin's crew flew the left wing position and the "Tourist" flew slot.

'The announcement that our target was Hamburg did not create a feeling of fear or desperation. Though I must admit I had a feeling of resignation and a deep seated conviction that this was to be my last mission. This feeling or premonition was so great that when a fellow Hoosier (resident of Indiana) said, "See you about 4:40 Frank," I replied, "Not me—we can't possibly make it over Hamburg for the third time." I am not sure what I expected, not death, unlike a high percentage of Eighth Air Force crew members. I did not have any doubt at any time that I would live through the Second World War. I believe this feeling was also shared by the other members of the crew. Leaving the briefing sessions, we caught our 6×6 transportation to our individual planes. This was to be our first mission in the new B-24L assigned to us as a replacement for the *Mrs*. We had taken this plane up for a shake-down flight a few days earlier and many requests for modifications were on our list. We wanted to make sure she deserved the honour of being christened *Never Mrs Too*. But we never flew the new 'L' model on a combat mission; she didn't check out on the 21st.

'The stand-by was *Dolly's Sister*. So that was the baby we took off in. Number four engine

Say When *of the 492nd BG being guarded by Swedish soldier at Bulltofta on 20 July 1944. Thirteen Liberators landed in Sweden that day.*

Below: Dual Sack *of the 448th BG which crashed at Bulltofta on 21 June 1944 and was later scrapped.*

began to act up before we reached the Channel. This was a new engine just installed and presumably slow timed. We had a run again, die again bout with number four all the way in to the target. I was not on intercom until the bomb run began. As radio operator I left my post and went to the bomb bay to check and see that no bombs hung up at the time of release. Upon arrival in the bomb bays from the flight deck I joined the rest of the crew on the intercom. This day, after reconnecting my oxygen mask, I connected to the intercom system just in time to hear H. A. Middleton, the navigator, ask, "You just feathered another engine?"

'I waited until all bombs had cleared the bays before inquiring how many engines we had lost. Whitehead informed me number two and number four were feathered and number three was losing power rapidly. Number three was on full throttle plus booster, manifold pressure had passed the red line, and was pulling in excess of 80 inches mercury pressure. He concluded by saying, "Incidentally, we're losing altitude at the rate of 2,000 feet per minute."

'Most air crews in trouble talked about going to Switzerland or Sweden, depending on their proximity to the target. Whitehead's next question to the crew was, "Shall we try to make Sweden?" The silence was deafening. After what seemed hours of waiting for someone to voice an opinion, I said "Let's go home, Boss." Whitehead informed us we had no more than 45 minutes in the air, and this would mean ditching in the North Sea. I replied, "In that case, let's shoot for Sweden." Middleton cut in and gave a heading for England followed by a heading for Sweden. In order to stay airborne, we began to throw everything we could overboard including ammunition, auxiliary power source and tuning units for my transmitter. During this mad house cleaning operation, James Taylor, the left waist gunner, called in, "I don't know if it makes any difference of not, but number three is on fire." His voice expressed no alarm or concern. I answered him by saying, "No, it didn't matter—just keep throwing out everything you can pry loose." I doubt if any of us realized what Taylor had said until we had eliminated all the weight we could and were beginning to level off. I can only speak for myself, when it did soak in, I was scared as hell.

'The "Tourist" luck continued to hold. As we levelled off the fire either burned itself out or was blown out. We didn't try to determine which was responsible, just gave our thanks. Herrman, the co-pilot, as he was accustomed to do, said, "The Big Boy still has us by the hand." We were down to approximately 2,000 feet by this time and nearing the Baltic Sea. With luck, we would be in Sweden before that 2,000 feet shrunk to zero.

'Our next problem was crossing into Sweden.

We were in no position to comply with international law requiring a damaged military plane to complete three complete circles, with bomb-bay doors open, wheels down and firing yellow flares before crossing the border of a neutral country. Any of these three procedures would have pulled us in. Luck still rode with us. We were below the Swedish radar and no one was aware of our presence at this time. Some anti-aircraft crews spotted us from their ground batteries and fired a few rounds but with no attempt to actually hit us. Our next cause for concern was a Scandinavian snowstorm which severely hampered us in our search for a place to set down.

'Everyone but Whitehead and Herrman had moved to the waist section, preparing for a crash landing or to bail out. Just as we emerged from the snowstorm, a Swedish fighter appeared on our right wing. The pilot began to signal that we were to drop our landing gears and open our bomb bays. We played it real dumb and waved back as if we thought he was just a one-man welcoming committee. Whitehead gave the order for us to bail out if we were not on the ground in five minutes. I asked his intention. He said, "We're riding her in." I replied, "The intercom has just gone dead, we can't hear a thing." He repeated his order. I spoke to the crew "No need to try the intercom—we can't hear a thing. Hope you can hear us. We have put up the crash belts and are ready to ride her in. Hope we are not alone. No need to waste any time trying to talk with us— just concentrate on setting the *Sister* down in one piece. Whitehead made a beautiful landing (as we knew he would) at Malmö. Just in time because *Dolly's Sister* had just about had it. The next thing I knew, a Swedish soldier (at least I hoped he was Swedish), was on the bomb-bay catwalk just in front of me. (I had headed for the flight deck.) The soldier had a sub-machine gun in the crook of his left arm and he sunk the end of the barrel in my stomach. Sticking out his right hand he said, "Welcome to Sweden!"

'The second soldier had a pistol pressed against Whitehead's temple and was motioning for him to taxi to the right. At this time, Whitehead asked me a very interesting question —preceded by a statement. "Tom, there's a Swedish soldier with a pistol at my head motioning me to taxi to the right. The second soldier is on the ground armed with a rifle pointed at me motioning for me to taxi to the left, which one should I obey?" I had problems of my own—but in my opinion, "Follow the request of the soldier nearest you." Slipping in under the radar screen had caught the troops at Malmö by surprise. We learned later that the soldiers were devoid of any ammo and were just as fearful we would come out shooting as we were that they might pull the trigger.

'Number two engine had had the oil rocker line shot out, number four gas lines had worked loose and the fire in number three was caused by the gasoline, intended for number four engine, running down the wing and burning, in number three's exhaust. The buckets of number three's supercharger were burned out due to the external fire. Battle damage, very little. We heard there were 268 German fighters in the air over Hamburg that 21 November. See what I mean about the "Luck of the Tourists."

'On the night of November 21, we had a wonderful meal including the first fresh milk since leaving the States five months earlier. We slept on mattresses filled with paper, comfortable but noisy. We also had a treat seeing Lieutenant Charles Huntoon's B-24H, *Hoo-Jive* which landed at Bulltofta on 25 August 1944. Seeing her sitting on Malmö airfield we knew her crew were safe.

'Northwardbound on the 23rd, with a stop in Stockholm, we were met by a representative of the State Department and a Warrant Officer representing the Eighth Air Force. We were told to sign a pledge not to try an escape from Sweden—which we did. The town of Falun, population about 19,000, was our destination for six weeks of detention—not nearly as bad as it sounds.'

Lieutenant Charles Christburg, the twenty-five-year-old bombardier in the crew recalls: 'We were interrogated, then fed at a Swedish officers' mess. We entrained for Stockholm with box lunches, including good beer that was a joy after months of English beer. We continued in the train to sporting lodges that were the internment camp near Falun, about 150 miles northwest of Stockholm. It was a great life. The lovely blonde girls of Falun were very sociable. There were good movies and eating and dancing places. We had our football, baseball and basketball teams and there was skiing and skating in the winter and sailboating and swimming in the warm weather.'

Frank Thomas continues: 'We were taken from Falun by bus to Humblebackens (Home in the Forest) which had been the home of a Swedish lumberman. A Mrs Johnson was in charge of all the domestic help. Sweden at that time was in the grip of a fuel shortage so we had hot water for only forty-five minutes each Friday. The limit on the supply of hot water required us to venture into Falun and visit the local bath house when we took our baths. As I recall we were limited to about two baths per week. We started with a shower then went into the steam-room—upon emerging from the steam bath we jumped into a pool of ice water: quite stimulating to say the least!

'H. A. Middleton the navigator, George Roby the nose-gunner, and Charles Rubbo the tail-gunner were returned to the States in December 1944. They were home by Christmas. Whitehead became C.O. at Falun. J. B. Taylor and Martin K. Boone, the waist gunners, were sent to Malmö and Västeras to

work on downed planes. Charles Christburg, Edward Herrman, Russell Harriman and I were sent to General Alfred A. Kessler's office at the American Legation in Stockholm. Christburg co-ordinated the work between the Air Attache's office and Count Bernadotte as it concerned movement of American internees in Sweden. Herrman worked with the General in other matters concerning Air Attache activities. In early 1945, Russ Harriman and I were ordered from Falun to Stockholm to join Air Attache personnel at the American Legation. Russ was assigned to work with Herrman and my dities consisted of control and distribution of Red Cross cigarettes to American personnel in Sweden and forwarding mail for Swedish internees and POWs in Germany. I also worked arrangements for getting released internees back to England, securing English visas, arranging for getting these men in ATC transport at Broma Field and clearance through Swedish Customs.

'Whitehead, Harriman and I, with two members from other crews, flew seven Liberators back to England during May, June, and July of 1945. In May 1945 we started up B-24H 42-7502, a 392nd Liberator which had landed at Orebo on 18 November 1943. This plane had not been started for over a year and we took her up for a "shake-down" flight. The following morning we left Västeras with enough gasoline to make it to Broma Field, Stockholm where we were fueled up. Whitehead, Harriman, and I together with two other internees, Lieutenant Miller as co-pilot and Lieutenant Robbins as navigator, left for England in the ex-392nd ship together with four other B-24s and a C-87 belonging to the Air Transport Command.

'One of the four Liberators was *Salvaged Sally* flown by Lieutenant Terry. Terry and his crew had been a B-24 test crew at Poccatella, Idaho but were assigned a B-17 after reaching the Eighth Air Force. The difference between feathering an engine electrically and hydraulically caused them to shake two engines loose from their mountings over Germany and they landed their B-17 in Sweden. *Salvaged Sally* was the compilation of four B-24s in Bulltofta. There is a strong possibility that the original plane was *Tondelayo*, a 492nd Liberator and one of eighteen which landed in Sweden on 20 June 1944. She flew like crazy in a nose-down attitude at about twenty miles an hour faster than any other B-24 we had flown, easy to handle in the air but hell to land!

'Whitehead, Harriman, and I picked her up in Malmö and flew her to Västeras; not bad when regulations required a crew of five (Harriman and I signed in for two positions each). We had no radios working and only one generator out of the four functioned. We landed at the ATC base at Metfield, England and were grounded for three days before we were allowed to fly the remaining ninety miles to Warton. We were

told she was not airworthy. Ha!

'We flew the last B-24 out on 12 July 1945. During our eight month stay in Sweden we made many friends and discovered that Swedish people are warm and friendly.'

Of the 110 American aircraft which crashed or landed in Sweden during the war, internees salvaged eighty-three for the return trip to England. Some of the rebuilt aircraft had few of their original parts, almost every nut and bolt being taken from cannibalized aircraft wrecked in crash landings. About 1,450 American airmen were technically POWs in Sweden during the war. They lived within their means, drawing flight pay and base pay. They also received a food and lodging allowance of 210 dollars a month, making a total of 482 dollars for a First Lieutenant. When travelling, the regular allowance of six dollars a day for maintenance was increased to thirteen dollars. But the downed airmen were goodwill ambassadors for America, ten at least married Swedish girls and others became engaged before the end of the war.

Right: *BOAC Liberators operated a flight from Leuchars, Scotland, to Stockholm during the war and brought back many valuable war materials, such as ballbearings, which were in short supply.*

70

Left: *Swedish personnel stop work on a J-22 fighter to watch a Focke-Wulf 'Condor' coming in to land at Broma Field, Stockholm. The transport made daily flights to the Swedish capital, often returning to Berlin with POW mail. On at least two occasions an American officer actually flew in the FW-200 to inspect American POWs in Germany.*

Above: *Salvaged Sally certainly lived up to her name, having been rebuilt from four different Liberators.*

Black Sheep in Wolves' Clothing

The wartime activities of the single engined RAF Lysanders dropping agents into occupied Europe is well known. By this method British agents, or 'Joes' as they were called, were ferried across the Channel and landed in France and the Low Countries. Agents, like Captain Harry Ree, Violette Szabo and Wing Commander Yeo-Thomas, the 'White Rabbit', entered occupied Europe with a brief to co-ordinate Resistance activity and instigate acts of sabotage. They reported directly to the British 'SOE' (Special Operations Executive) in London which was responsible for the co-ordination of Resistance operations with Allied Strategical requirements.

The SOE grew from humble beginnings, reaching the peak of its achievements on D-Day. By December 1944, 293 agents and other personnel had been ferried to France and over 500 brought back. At first the British used Whitleys and later Halifaxes. In February 1942, 138 and 161 Squadrons (Special Duties) had began operations from secret airfields at Tempsford near the A1 in Cambridge and Newmarket.

On a much bigger scale, the American OSS (Office of Strategic Services) was introduced to supplement SOE operations. The Americans were unprepared for Resistance support but by 1942 OSS was functioning very effectively under the dynamic leadership of Colonel William Donovan. In September that year the joint Ango-American SOE-SO was formed and the Americans began participating in the planning of operations in many north-west European countries.

The major USAAF effort to supply the Resistance movements in Europe began under the code name 'Carpetbagger' which someone had lifted from the annals of the American Civil War. Once again it was the Liberator which was selected for these operations because of its long range and capacious fuselage. Ball turrets were removed and replaced with cargo hatches, nicknamed 'Joe Holes' through which the secret agents or 'Joes' dropped. To facilitate bail-outs the hole had a metal shroud inside the opening.

If the Liberator did not have a ball turret, a hole was made there.

Plywood covered the floors and blackout curtains graced the waist windows. The outer skins of the Liberators were painted in a special non-glare black paint. Blister windows were installed to give the pilots greater visibility. If the model had a nose turret, it was removed. A greenhouse was fashioned to allow the bombardier a good view of the drop zone and to enable him to carry out pilotage for the navigator. Exhaust suppressors or flame

dampers were fitted to the engines to stifle the tell-tale exhaust flames. Guns located on both sides of the waist were removed, leaving only the top and rear turrets for protection. In flight the entire aircraft was blacked out except for a small light in the navigator's compartment. After conversion the black B-24s were practically undetectable at night.

However, the Liberator was a heavy aircraft; just under sixteen tons, so only C-47s, RAF Hudsons and Lysanders actually landed on the improvised landing strips in western Europe. Even so, they often bogged down. To aid in navigation 'Gee' was installed in the black B-24s. Although limited in range to approximately 400 miles, with a little care in reading, it was very accurate. A US Navy system for 'homing', effective up to a range of 100 miles, was also installed. Radar altimeters of extreme accuracy were used when making drops.

Personnel were drawn from the 4th and 22nd Squadrons of the 479th Anti-Submarine Group, which had been disbanded in August 1943. They were selected because of their experience in long navigational patrols at night. Operations were mounted from Tempsford under RAF guidance from January 1944, while administered by the 482nd Bombardment Group (Pathfinder) at Alconbury, Cambridgeshire, until 27 February 1944. That month,

several of the 'Carpetbagger' Liberators were moved to Watton. On 28 March 1944 the 'Carpetbaggers' were established as the 801st Provisional Bombardment Group. On 13 August that year it was redesignated the 492nd Bombardment Group (Heavy) taking the designation from the recently disbanded Group of that name. The Eighth Air Force had activated the 36th and 406th Bombardment Squadrons in November 1943 and attached them as a sub-group to the 482nd Bomb Group (Pathfinder) at Alconbury. The 36th and 406th Squadrons (redesignated the 856th and 858th Squadrons respectively on 13 August 1944) only operated from Watton while the main part of the unit, commanded by Lieutenant-Colonel Clifford J. Heflin, had its headquarters at and operated from Harrington, Buckinghamshire.

Harrington, like Tempsford, was completely sealed off from the public and its 3,000 personnel were under strict orders not to reveal the true nature of the black Liberators. Any inquisitive local or inquiring civilian in the 'liberty' towns of Leicester and Northampton were fobbed off with stories of 'Pathfinders'. Not even administrative officers and crewmen were told officially although they had a very good idea.

By the war's end the 492nd had dropped 4,500 tons of equipment and had landed hundreds of agents on the Continent. In the

An extremely rare view of a 'Carpetbagger' Liberator taking off from Prestwick.

A black B-24 of the 'Carpetbaggers' takes off on another 'Joe' drop.

Operations rooms at Harrington and Tempsford large wall maps pinpointed with small flags denoted every landing ground and reception field in Europe from the tip of Norway to the far flung corners of Germany and Austria. While original 'Carpetbagger' personnel were drawn from the anti-submarine squadrons, further crews came from B-24 groups in East Anglia. One of these was Major Edgar F. Townsend who had originally been assigned to the 453rd Bomb Group at Old Buckenham. He recalls:

'The crew of four officers and four airmen were alerted or awakened [the crew may have flown the night before] at 11.00-11.30 hours for the noon meal. At 13.00 hours the crews reported to the Operations room for briefing. Each crew was then assigned its target by the Squadron C.O. or the Squadron Operations Officer. The crews that flew the previous night were normally assigned the short flights and the long flights were given to fresh crews. The navigator of each crew plotted the target on the flight chart to determine the general direction of the flight.

'Intelligence briefing consisted of the latest information regarding the location of the battle line, possible night fighter activity, new enemy tactics and the location and size of anti-aircraft guns. The details were plotted on a large map for the navigators and bombardiers to copy onto their flight charts. These charts were large scale and showed many more landmarks than normal charts including the shape of woods and forests. Charts were also overlaid with 'Gee' lines so that all navigation could be done on one chart.

'Radio briefing consisted of the correct IFF setting, codes and frequencies to be used depending on the time and area into which the flight was to be made. Normally the IFF was used up to the battle line and then turned off. Radio was monitored but no transmissions were normally made until craft were re-crossing the English Channel.

'Weather briefing consisted of the detailed forecast for each general operational area. Crews were given wind directions and velocities at various altitudes up to 10,000 feet, also details of the type and amount of clouds, and the position and movements of frontal systems.

'After all the briefings were completed the crews then set up their own flight plans. First a course was determined from the base to the point of departure from England. After crossing the coastline, a zigzag course was used to the target to avoid known enemy anti-aircraft guns. By an unwritten law, the legs of the zig-zag course were limited to thirty nautical miles to prevent an enemy night fighter from lining up from behind to make an attack. Another zig-zag course was set up for the return flight to the enemy coastline.

'Operations over enemy-held territory had to be conducted in the period of total darkness, which during summer was often as little as five or six hours in northern latitudes. Once the flight path was established, total flight time was worked out using the forecast wind speeds for the selected altitude. Each crew then turned in its forecast flight plan and Group set up the take-off times. At least ten minutes was allowed between planes entering the same area and those with the longest flights went in first.

'When the target was given to the crew, they were also told the recognition signal they would receive from the ground. This could be three lights in a row, or two lights in a row with an extra light showing the wind direction. These lights could be torches or fires on the ground. When the target area was identified, the pilot lined up into the wind and approached at slow speed flying at 400 feet (600 feet if 'Joes' were being dropped) using the radar altimeter. The bombardier controlled the time of drop. When the first light was immediately below he releaed the canisters from the bomb bay and signalled the drop man in the waist to kick out the large packages. A stop signal was given over the last light and if all the material had not been dropped, a second pass was necessary. This, of course, increased the danger to both the plane and the personnel on the ground.'

Few landing fields had radios to guide in the Liberators so most of the drops were made using hand-held lights. Agents of all nationalities were dropped and some were anti-Nazi Germans. One agent even took with him a gramophone record denouncing Laval which was to be surreptitiously inserted into a Vichy radio programme. On the afternoon before their flight the 'Joes' would be taken to Tempsford and Harrington by car. Intelligence officers searched them thoroughly to make sure they carried no giveaway objects like American cigarettes or London transport tickets. At the secret bases, tailors fitted out each agent in the appropriate clothes. One anti-Nazi agent made three trips dressed as a German officer and two as a German civilian.

The mission were fraught with danger and on one occasion a B-24 returned to Harrington with over 1,000 bullet holes in it after being tracked by German radar and attacked by two night fighters. Sometimes the Germans constructed dummy landing strips but the cargo seldom fell into enemy hands because they could not flash the correct signals. Sometimes accidents happened on board the Liberators themselves. On the night of 27 April 1944 a black Liberator, The Worry Bird, piloted by First Lieutenant George Ambrose, took off for a dropping mission to France. Jim Monier was flying his first 'Carpetbagger' mission. While pushing out a parachute package through the 'Joe Hole', he slipped and fell through the opening himself. The Liberator was extremely low at the time and it is believed he rode the parachute down. Some Frenchmen found him but he was so badly injured they had no choice but to turn him over to the Germans for medical help. He returned to America after the war. Only two men from the eight-man crew (not counting Monier) survived when the B-24 was later shot down in flames near St Cyr de Valorges in the early hours of 28 April. George Henderson and Jim Heddleson hid from the Germans for two days and were finally picked up by the French Resistance. After taking part in night time raids with the Maquis, they returned to England two months later.

Just prior to and shortly after D-Day, special 'Jedburgh' liaison teams in uniform were dropped into enemy occupied territory to control and direct Resistance operations. It was felt that as D-Day approached co-ordination was needed between the Underground movements and the Allied invasion force. One hundred three-man teams, or 'Jedburghs', consisting of two officers and a sergeant radio operator, were dropped by the 'Carpetbaggers'. British, French, and American nationalities were all represented and did much to enhance the successful D-Day assaults.

But not all 'Carpetbagger' operations were based in the East of England and not all

involved France and the Low Countries. Early in 1944 about 2,000 Norwegians were in training in Sweden, partly under the direction of Swedish officers. The Norwegian Government in Exile wanted to airlift this 'pocket army' to England and thence to the Norwegian base near Toronto, Canada for further training. General Carl Spaatz of the American Strategic Air Force selected Norwegian-born Colonel Bernt Balchen for the task, code-named the 'Sonnie' project. Balchen had piloted Admiral Richard E. Byrd over the South Pole in 1929 and had made several flights over the North Pole and Antarctica during the early 1930s. In 1931 Balchen became a naturalized American subject. Besides his experience gained on the Polar flights, Balchen knew almost every inch of the mountainous Norwegian terrain having been a post-war Operations Manager and President of Norwegian Airlines—DNL.

Colonel Balchen was designated as representative of the Commanding General, United States Strategic Air Forces in Europe. He was allocated the RAF base at Leuchars, near Aberdeen in Scotland from which to mount the project. The consent of both the Swedish and British Governments was required before American aircraft could fly in and out of Sweden, a neutral country. The British authorities were worried over the effect American wartime routes might have on post-war British airline interests in Scandinavia and tried to prevent the inauguration of the project. However it went ahead and Balchen helped smooth over the political implications with the help of his many contacts in Scandinavia. Through his intervention, other nationalities, including American internees, were also evacuated.

To maintain Sweden's neutrality, all flights were put on a civilian footing and the Liberators flew unarmed and carried no military markings. The Swedish Air Ministry co-operated and informed the Americans of any German fighter activity along its borders. As an additional precaution, any German

Crew of Screwball. Back row left to right: 1st Lieutenant Edgar F. Townsend (navigator), 1st Lieutenant Samuel Godsmith (pilot), 2nd Lieutenant George A. Procuniar (bombardier), 2nd Lieutenant Earl E. Bitzer (co-pilot). Front row: Unknown. The flash eliminators on the guns can be clearly seen and the nose has a faired off greenhouse.

A 'Carpetbagger' interior after modification at BAD-2 Warton.

shipping movements out of Norwegian ports were radioed by the Norwegian Resistance to Stockholm.

The 'Sonnie' project began with five war-weary Liberators and only six crews. Gradually it was enlarged to include five C-87s and eleven flight crews. During the period from March to December 1944, 110 round trips were made with the loss of only one aircraft. Operations were carried out under extremely dangerous weather conditions. Coupled with this, Swedish airfields were really unsuitable for heavy aircraft such as the Liberator and the flights were subject to the constant danger of Luftwaffe attack. Colonel Balchen flew the first three 'Sonnie' missions himself.

The Swedish authorities had permitted the arrival and departure of only three Liberators a day at Bromma Airport in Stockholm. 'Sonnie' B-24s were assigned three corridors across Swedish territory, each only about twenty miles wide. Any Liberator which strayed outside these corridors would be fired on by Swedish anti-aircraft batteries after one warning shot. A further problem for the air crews was that when they reached Sweden, the acute fuel shortage meant that each aircraft was only allowed 300-400 gallons of gasoline for the return trip to Scotland. After a normal run, aircraft landed in Britain with only approximately two hours' fuel reserve, leaving no margin for error.

The Air Transport Command personnel changed into civilian clothes before leaving their aircraft in Sweden and carried passports and civilian flying licences. Nonetheless they were soon identified by the Germans and their hotel rooms were often ransacked for information on the secret corridors and take-off times. It was estimated that about 250 Luftwaffe night fighters were based in southern Norway but the B-24 crews made long detours northwards before crossing Norwegian territory into Sweden.

'The 'Sonnie' project was so successful that ultimately 3,016 passengers were evacuated including 1,847 Norwegian trainees and 965 American internees. The remainder included French, Soviet and Dutch Government officials. On one occasion the entire personnel of the Norwegian Government in Exile were flown to Sweden. On the return flights, upwards of thirty-five passengers were uncomfortably crammed into the hold of the Liberators.

Meanwhile, 'Carpetbagger' operations continued from East Anglia. By the end of May 1944 there were four squadrons equipped with the black-painted Liberators. That month SOE-SO became Special Force Headquarters (SFHQ) responsible to General Eisenhower at Supreme Headquarters, Allied Expeditionary Force (SHAEF) for all Resistance operations within the Supreme Commander's sphere of responsibility. Additional Liberators were ac-

quired from the 467th Heavy Bombardment Group at Rackheath, Norfolk and sent to the 801st Provisional Bomb Group.

In early May 1944 Lieutenant William Dillon and his crew were one of the 788th Squadron crews at Rackheath sent to RAF Tempsford for transitional training on night missions with the 'Carpetbaggers'. He recalls: 'None of us knew what we were getting into but everybody looked forward in anticipation to these night missions because some of our high altitude day-light missions had been pretty rough. Of course we found later that some of the night missions were pretty rough too. When we got through night training we were posted to Harrington and the 801st. The pilot, navigator and bombardier all took separate flights for orientation over the Continent. We started our missions as a crew in the latter part of May 1944.

'We flew mostly between 6,500 and 8,000 feet trying to stay out of reach of ack-ack or light machine-gun fire. In bad weather we had to rely on the navigator's dead reckoning. In good weather we could rely on navigation and pilotage. If the pilot was flying then his co-pilot did the navigation and vice versa. 'Gee' was very beneficial but by the time we hit the continental coast the Germans had the system jammed. Over the dropping zones we could talk to the patriots on the improvised landing strips by using the 'S' Phone. It would have helped if we could have spoken the language.'

When the 'Carpetbagger' crews dropped agents they were usually dropped from 600 feet. Staff-Sergeant Max B. Rufner was the dispatcher on Bill Dillon's crew and recalls that the 'Joe' drops were the 'special nights':

'I don't think it occurred more than three or four times that we had people to drop. I recall one night we had a lady radio operator. The poor girl was sick all the way over. We found the target and received the proper signal so out she went. She was a pretty brave girl I thought but I couldn't tell what she looked like because she was all bundled up in paratrooper's gear.'

During July 1944 the four 'Carpetbagger' squadrons flew a total of 397 sorties, dropping thousands of containers, packages and bundles of leaflets and sixty-two 'Joes'. Among the crews who took part in missions that month was Edgar Townsend: 'One night in July 1944 we were crossing the English coast in the vicinity of Brighton on a south-easterly course. At the same time an RAF Halifax flying on an easterly course and about twenty feet below crossed right under our nose. Even in the black of night with just a little moon we could see the markings on the fuselage and tail. Mid-air collision was probably one of the greatest fears of night flying personnel. I never looked out again except during the drops over the target.

'One of the long missions was made south east of Bordeaux about 100 miles from the Franco-Spanish border. On the way home we crossed the French coast at 5,000 feet just south of Bordeaux. The enemy started hunting our plane with three searchlights criss-crossing the sky several times. Finally one caught us for a few seconds and moved on still searching. I feel sure they were unable to see the plane even in the light. My bombardier later stated that the light was so bright he could have read a paper.

From January to May 1944 twenty-five black Liberators were lost on missions and eight others so severely damaged by ground fire that they had to be salvaged. Full-scale 'Carpetbagger' operations from Watton finally ceased in September 1944 and the black Liberators were transferred to Leuchars.

In June 1944 the Norwegian section of the OSS sent an urgent plea for help to General Carl A. Spaatz, Commanding General of the USSTAF. He immediately directed Bernt Balchen's highly successful unit to begin parachuting arms, supplies and secret agents into Norway. Six war-weary Liberators, painted dull black, and seven veteran crews were detached for the Norwegian operations. Top secret navigational equipment was installed in the B-24s and flame responders were fitted to the machine-guns. Flame dampers were placed over the exhausts and the ball turrets were removed. Because of this the operation was christened the 'Ball Project'.

The 'Ball Project' began on 17 July 1944 with Balchen as command pilot and continued until September that year. These flights were particularly dangerous because of the low altitudes required for a successful drop. The ATC crews had to pinpoint their targets in order to avoid having their supplies or agents dropped into the clutches of the Germans. Underground groups had to be informed in advance of the missions and assembled at a predetermined rendezvous. After flying across the North Sea at minimum altitudes and crossing the coastline at approximately 6,000 feet, the Liberators would make their final run in at 1,000 feet and drop their supplies or agents squarely into the selected area. The supplies were supposed to be dropped within an area of 100 yards of fires lit by the Norwegians. Earl Zimmerman, who had flown with the 389th at Ploesti and on combat missions in the ETO was one of the crew members to serve on the 'Ball Project'. He recalls: 'We always got the word from Colonel Balchen if the mission was on or not. He would come out, look at the sky and say, "All right, we go." Sometimes we would fly a few 360s to confuse German tracking stations and once in a while we would get caught in searchlights but somehow or other the Norwegians had always obtained the colours of the day and we would fire off the correct flare and the lights would be turned off immediately. On all our drops we threw out candy and cigarettes in addition to the official containers. But we had our scares. On one occasion a very bright light crossed us going from right to left. We were at about 6,000 feet. We didn't know

what to think of it but after the war someone came up with the theory that it might have been a jet.'

In addition to the candy and cigarettes, the 'Ball Project' crews carried with them copies of British and American newspapers. Underground members later reported that they took special delight in leaving them in the hotels of Bergen, Oslo, and Trondheim for the Gestapo to find during their constant probings and searches.

The six Liberators of 'Ball Project' dropped a total of 120 tons of cargo and OSS personnel mostly in southern and central Norway during their sixty-seven missions. Forty-one of these missions were successfully credited but enemy opposition was fierce. The Luftwaffe made an appearance on fifteen of the missions and although the fighters caused no immediate damage, bad weather and other operational hazards resulted in the loss of two Liberators and twelve men killed. Among them was Lieutenant Colonel Keith Allen, who had flown the first 'Sonnie' mission in March 1944. Ken Armstrong, a member of the ground staff, recalls: 'Apparently Lieutenant Colonel Allen's Liberator was fired upon in error by the Russians. After they were hit Allen ordered the crew to abandon the aircraft. He stayed with the plane and was killed in the crash. The other members of the crew later returned to Leuchars after they were picked up by the Russians.'

During the final phase of the 'Ball Project' a unit of American soldiers was parachuted into Hitler's northern redoubt in Bavaria. In September 1944 when the project was finally terminated, the task of supplying the Norwegian Underground reverted to the Eighth Air Force and later the RAF.

As a consequence of the wartime 'Carpetbagger' operations, the first American commercial routes between the United States and Sweden were opened. The first scheduled flight from Presque Island via Meeks Field took place on 1 June 1945. American military aircraft operated a round trip once a week until late August 1945 when American Export Airlines took over.

A partially painted 'Carpetbagger' which came to grief after over-shooting the runway.

BAD NO2 29 JUNE 45 2749-1 B-24 42 5060
(CONFIDENTIAL)

Bomber Support Liberators

Bombing missions during the Second World War frequently made the headlines but support units, involved in radio counter-measures (RCM) and night leaflet operations in Europe and the Far East, are rarely mentioned. Some of these units carried out duties equally valuable and frequently more important than the activities of the bomber units, although even the crews who participated in bomber support missions sometimes took a lot of convincing.

As the protagonists progressed from the pre-war technological doldrums into an increasingly electronically orientated war more and more radio counter-measures had to be devised. The British were quick to realize this, having experienced German radio aids like 'Knickebein' during the Battle of Britain and the necessity to jam them. But it was not until late in 1943 that the RAF decided to create its own radio counter-measures group.

On 8 November No. 100 Group (RAF) Bomber Support Group was formed under the command of Air Commodore E. B. Addison to embrace both air and ground radio counter-measures (RCM) and provide a long range fighter offensive against German air defences. Initially its Headquarters was at Radlett in Hertfordshire. In December 1943 it moved to West Raynham in Norfolk and on 18 January 1944 was finally located at Bylaugh Hall near East Dereham in Norfolk. Using Halifaxes and Mosquitoes and later Fortresses and Liberators these operations were so successful that the United States also took an interest. On 19 January 1944 the 803rd Bombardment Squadron (Provisional) was activated at Sculthorpe, Norfolk, equipped with B-17s. The RAF supplied and helped to install the equipment and conducted the necessary training until mid-May, when the squadron, now re-designated the 36th Bomb Squadron, moved to Oulton in Norfolk to begin operations. By August 1944 the 36th had exchanged its Fortresses for the more accommodating Liberators, capable of carrying up to as many as thirty jamming sets. The Liberators' long range made them ideal aircraft for the task and the 36th used them for the remainder of the war. On 14 August 1944 the Squadron's eleven B-24Hs and Js and two B-17s were transferred to Cheddington, where they operated principally on daylight missions.

The hardstands at Oulton meanwhile were filled by more black B-24s and B-17s belonging to No. 223 Squadron (RAF) which was formed on 23 August originally as a second 'Jostle' jamming unit in 100 Group. However in mid-July 1944 the wreckage of a German rocket, thought to be a V2, was flown to England for scrutiny at RAE Farnborough. The missile had landed in Sweden after a test firing from the German research station at Peenemünde on the other side of the Baltic. Immediately urgent steps were taken to develop a counter-measure and 'Jostle' equipment was subsequently modified to the 'Big Ben' configuration. However, the wreckage in the hands of the RAE Farnborough belonged not to the V2 but the Wasserfall anti-aircraft missile. Unfortunately this was not realized until after the war.

No. 223 Squadron was equipped with second-hand B-24 Liberators from the Eighth Air Force. Many of these had already seen widespread service and some had accumulated

more than 350 flying hours. The Eighth Air Force repaid the RAF's help in getting 803 Squadron operational by servicing the Liberators at Watton, Norfolk, and generally assisting with the Squadron's formation. Such was the urgency of the threat posed by the V2s, that crews drawn from Coastal Command Liberator OTUs became operational after only fifteen hours' flying training. Sergeant Don Prutton, a flight engineer, was among the first to join the special duties squadron at Oulton:

'In the early hours of 3 September 1944 myself and a party of sergeant flight engineers fresh from technical school at St. Athan, South Wales, arrived slightly puzzled at Norwich railway station. We gathered that 100 Group, to which the newly-formed 223 Squadron belonged, was a 'Special' group; we would be on 'Special duties' and would be joined by 'special operators'. We shared the airfield with 214 Squadron, similarly employed, using B-17 Fortresses. We did out first operational flight on 2 October 1944 in *B-Baker* We patrolled in daylight off the Dutch coast at about 20,000 feet, hoping to spot a V2 on its way up from its launching pad. We carried two special operators who were doing mysterious things with radar jamming devices but security was so good that even the rest of the crew did not have the slightest idea of what they were up to.

'These daylight patrols came to an end in October and we began our real work which involved night operations with the rest of Bomber Command. These operations were of two distinct types. In the first, two or three of our aircraft would accompany the main bomber stream and then circle above the target; the special operators used their transmitters, in particular 'Jostle', to jam the German radar defences while the Lancasters and Halifaxes unloaded their bombs. Then everyone headed for home. Our friends in 214 Squadron seemed to do more of these target operations than 223 Squadron. My own crew did a small number of these but the majority of our operations were of the second type, the 'Window' spoofs. The object of these 'Window' raids was to confuse the enemy as to the intended target. There was a radar screen created by other aircraft patrolling in a line roughly north to south over the North Sea and France. A group of us, perhaps eight aircraft, would emerge through this screen scattering 'Window' (long strips of metal foil) to give the impression to the German radar operators that a large bomber force was heading for, say, Hamburg. Then, when the Germans were concentrating their night fighters in that area, the real bomber force would appear through the screen and bomb a totally different target, perhaps Düsseldorf. After several nights, when the Germans had become used to regarding the first group of aircraft as a dummy raid, the drill was reversed; the genuine bombers would appear first and with luck be ignored by the German defences, who would instead concentrate on the second

Photographs of RAF RCM Liberators are rare. This one shows a B-24 of 223 Squadron: Left to right: Flight Sergeant Benn Buff (beam gunner), Flying Officer Joe Doolin (wireless operator), Sergeant Murdo McIver (beam gunner), Flight Lieutenant Gordon Bremness (pilot), Flying Officer Hal Booth (navigator), Sergeant Sam Leach (tail gunner), Sergeant Roy Storr (mid upper gunner), Sergeant Don Prutton (flight engineer). Note the sealed Emerson nose turret painted over black and the 'Window' chute protruding from the bomb-bay below the flame damper under the nacelle.

bunch, which was of course our 'Window' spoof. So we rang the changes, sometimes going in first, sometimes last, in an attempt to cause maximum confusion to the enemy, dissipation of his resources and reduction in our own bomber losses.

'The 'Window' was carried in the rear half of the bomb bay which was floored and separated by doors from the rest of the aircraft so it was impossible to have a low light on. The rear bomb doors were fixed shut, unlike the front ones which were still operational and were the means of getting into and out of the aircraft. The 'Window' was wrapped in brown paper bundles about a foot long and perhaps two or three inches across. Each bundle had a string loop and the idea was that as you pushed the bundle down the specially installed chute near the floor of the compartment you held on to the string loop. This ripped the brown paper wrapper and as the bundle was drawn out by the slipstream the contents were scattered on the night air.

'It was normally a two-man job, usually the flight engineer and one of the beam gunners, and was quite hard work bearing in mind we were in bulky flying suits, helmets and oxygen masks. At the pre-flight briefing the rate of discharge was stipulated: it was to start at, say, forty bundles a minute and then as we approached our 'target' it must increase to perhaps sixty a minute! In practice we knelt or sat on the floor surrounded by the mountain of bundles and when the navigator gave the word the plane started weaving gently and we started pushing the stuff out fast. When the time came to increase the rate we just went even faster but whether it was correct or not we never knew.

'We normally used Type 'A'. We also carried a few bundles of Type 'C' and always made sure we knew where these were because Type 'C' was for our own protection. If the anti-aircraft fire started getting too close for comfort we would sling out some Type 'C' and miraculously the flak would drop behind us. I believe our 'Window' operations were reasonably successful; certainly our bomber losses were greatly reduced in the last months of the war. I think we also helped the Germans use up their aviation fuel.

'On the night of 10/11th February 1945 there were twelve of us against the Luftwaffe. We had a briefing in the afternoon but weather was clamping down all over Britain and the bombing plans were later 'scrubbed'. However two crews each from 214 and 233 Squadrons were put on standby. At 9 pm we had another briefing and learned that as East Anglia seemed likely to remain clear it had been decided that 100 Group should deny the German forces a night off. So just after midnight a dozen assorted aircraft from the Group took off on a 'Window' raid to Krefeld in the Ruhr. It was bright moonlight above the clouds; the occasional searchlight filtered through and at one stage a fighter tailed us a for a few minutes but other than this we saw no enemy activity and all returned safely. In all we felt the trip was probably a waste of time, but when we landed at about 5 am we were greeted by our Commanding Officer, Wing Commander Burnell, with the news that 'half the German air force' had been up looking for us. We later had a message from the A.O.C. confirming that the operation had been 'an unqualified success and in every manner achieved its object'.

'Our own losses were comparatively light. Of the six flight engineers I arrived with, four survived, but in the Squadron as a whole the survival rate was probably slightly higher than this. It used to be said sometimes that we were in more danger from the unserviceability of the aircraft than from enemy action.'

In June 1945, Exrcise Post Mortem, was carried out by the British to evaluate the effectiveness of RAF 'jamming' and 'spoof' operations on the German early warning radar system. Simulated attacks were made by aircraft from four RAF groups including 100 Group, the EW radar being manned by Allied personnel on this occasion. The exercise lasted until early July and proved conclusively that the counter measures had been a great success.

The British attempted to introduce jamming devices in the Mediterranean but priority always fell to the European theatre. The American 15th Air Force in Italy was well equipped with RCM before the end of the war in Europe.

While RAF Liberators in the Mediterranean encountered reasonably strong flak defences during their night offensives, their sister squadrons in the Far East had little need for electronic counter-measures. Towards the end of the war in the Far East five RAF Liberator squadrons were operating against the Japanese in daylight but the enemy was equipped with only primitive radar equipment. None the less the RAF decided that a special flight should be formed to monitor enemy W/T and R/T transmissions and plot his radar stations. A special ELINT (Electronic Intelligence) flight was activated under the control of 159 Squadron and began operations in September 1944. ELINT missions were carried out until early January 1945 when the Special Flight began dropping leaflets.

On the night of 31 January 1945 Flight Sergeant Stanley James Woodbridge, a wireless operator with 159 Squadron, was personally selected by his Squadron Commander to fly with a crack crew on an important mission to pinpoint the location of certain Japanese radar installations in Bangkok, Mandalay and Rangoon.

The operation was successfully completed and the Liberator was turning for home at 3.10 am when it suddenly developed engine trouble and the skipper gave the order to bail out. Incredibly, six of the eight crew members

An ELINT Liberator
*prepares to take off from its
base in India.*

managed to parachute into the same area and reunite on the ground. The other two airmen, who were in the rear of the Liberator, were never seen again and are believed to have perished in the crash. The six survivors—two officers and four NCOs—started to trek towards the coast in the hope of finding a boat and putting out to sea where Air Sea Rescue might be able to locate them as Flight Sergeant Woodbridge had managed to send a last minute SOS. The Bay of Bengal was combed repeatedly for four days.

Meanwhile the airmen came upon a small village and offered the head man a large sum if he would get them a small boat. He agreed and told them to hide. For two hours the six men waited, confident that they would soon be back with their friends in the squadron. But when the headman returned he brought with him a force of Japanese soldiers.

The six airmen were conveyed down the Irrawaddy River to the Bassein district where they were handed over to the Japanese 55th Engineering Regiment. Lieutenant-Colonel Murayama, the regiment's Commanding Officer instructed Lieutenant Okami, his civil defence officer, to question the six British airmen. The skipper was the first to be interrogated. He produced a document on which was written, in Japanese, an extract from the Geneva Convention stating that prisoners of war need only tell their captors their name, rank and serial number. Japan was ostensibly a signatory of the convention, although it had been no respecter of the rights of those prisoners who were forced to build the Burma railway. When the skipper refused to reveal the name of his base he was severely beaten for half an hour. The second officer, the navigator, was then questioned but was not beaten because the interrogator was only interested in learning the identity of the wireless-operator. All four NCOs were beaten, but when the interrogator recognized that Woodbridge was the wireless operator, it was he who bore the brunt of the tortures.

Woodbridge was asked to reveal his codes and wavelengths, to give technical details of the equipment carried in the Liberator and tell what link he had with operators on the ground who were responsible for providing details of Japanese targets. Woodbridge steadfastly refused to reveal one scrap of information to his captors. After the first interrogations, the two officers were taken away in the middle of the night to Japanese headquarters in Rangoon for a more detailed interrogation. When the British overran Rangoon these two officers were found in gaol and released. But the fate of the four RAF airmen was sealed. The beatings began again and continued for four hours. Fists, bamboo canes, and swords in their sheaths were used on the badly bruised Woodbridge. One of the soldiers, a ju-jitsu expert, threw the gallant airman around for some considerable time and at intervals another officer, Lieutenant Kanno, encouraged his soldiers to kick the defenceless airman where he lay. Eventually Kanno's patience was exhausted with the realization that no amount of torture would force the courageous airman to speak. Woodbridge was then told he was to meet the same fate as his colleagues, who had already been executed.

As Stanley Woodbridge reached the spot where his three fellow crew members had been executed he paid a silent tribute to them. They had been forced to dig their own grave, a trench about two and a half feet deep and long enough to take four, not three bodies. After digging the trench all three men were made to stand in line, then a Japanese officer, Lieutenant Matsui, invited his soldiers to kick and beat them. The airmen were then brought to the edge of the trench, blindfolded and forced to squat. Matsui ordered two prisoners to be beheaded and then Kanno ordered a corporal to behead the third airman. All the bodies were subjected to bayoneting. Woodbridge was beheaded by one of Kanno's fellow officers, Lieutenant Okami, and pushed into the grave. He died defiant.

In 1947 at the war crimes trial in Rangoon, Kanno, Okami, and a corporal were convicted and hanged. Lieutenant-Colonel Murayama was sentenced to death. It was established that Lieutenant Matsui had been killed in action during the Japanese retreat from Burma.

On 28 September 1948 it was announced that Stanley James Woodbridge had been post-humously awarded the George Cross.

Mediterranean Missions

Of all the theatres of operations in which the B-24 served during the Second World War, only in the Mediterranean did it see such widespread and diversified service with both the RAF and the USAAF. As early as December 1941 No. 108 Squadron, then based in Egypt and equipped with Wellington bombers, received four Liberator Mark IIs, which had been originally intended for France. These unarmed Liberators remained in Egypt until it was decided that 108 Squadron should use them to convert fully from Wellingtons to Liberators. However, after they had been fitted with Boulton & Paul gun turrets, and cannon, the plan to convert the whole Squadron to Liberators was abandoned and only two were ever used for bombing operations. Some others which had been used for conversion training were modified for supply-dropping duties.

The four Liberator Mark IIs operated as a separate flight from the rest of 108 Squadron, which continued using Wellingtons right up to November 1942. For a time the flight operated from Palestine. William Foulkes, a fitter from 108 Squadron, recalls: 'Keeping the Liberators flying was a problem. Just prior to the Battle of El Alamein we were operating from a base on the Cairo/Alexandria road about sixty miles from Alamein. Two of the Liberators had suspect engines so the one that was nearest its next major overhaul was cannibalized and its engines used on the other aircraft. The cowlings, however, did not fit properly on their new mountings and had to be fastened with nuts and bolts and even wire!'

In May 1942, twenty-three B-24Ds of the Halverson Detachment took off from Morrison Field, Florida, but by this time a critical situation had developed in the land war in Libya. By early June the HALPRO Detachment had arrived safely at Fayid on the Great Bitter Lake near the Suez Canal and it was decided that they would first strike at the oilfields at Ploesti in Rumania.

Halverson's Detachment never got to the Far East. Throughout June 1942 the small force bombed enemy installations in Tobruk and Benghazi during the backwards and forwards war between the British Desert Rats and Rommel's Afrika Korps. By the end of June the Eighth Army had retreated to El Alamein and General Lewis Brereton had been summoned from India with 'such heavy bombers as were available'. After their mission of 1 July 1942 the Halverson Detachment was re-formed as the First Provisional Bomb Group and their numbers swelled by several of Brereton's B-17s from India.

From June until the end of October 1942 the Group attacked Axis convoys in the Mediterranean and airfields in Greece and Crete. On 1 November 1942 the 1st Provisional Group was absorbed into the 376th Bombardment Group which arrived at Lydda with its desert-pink Liberators. It marked a growing American prominence in the Mediterranean. In July 1942 the first Liberators belonging to the 98th Bomb Group had arrived in Palestine and were based at Ramat David near Haifa. By 4 November Rommel's forces had been crushed at El Alamein and were on the retreat. That month General Brereton was authorized to activate the 9th Air Force with Brigadier General Patrick W. Timberlake commanding Ninth Bomber Command.

As a result of Operation Torch in November 1942, RAF Eastern Air Command had been formed under Air Marshal Sir William Welsh primarily to support the British First Army in its advance on Tunis. Seven weeks after the landings Welsh was able to deploy about 450 aircraft, and Major General James Doolittle's newly created 12th Air Force about 1,250 for the North African campaign.

By the end of 1942 the growing success of Eastern Air Command could not hide the fact that there was still no integrated direction of the Allied Air Forces in North Africa. While EAC and Doolittle's 12th Air Force continued to act independently, the position was further complicated by the presence of Brereton's 9th AF which was also playing a vital part in the North African campaign. Air Marshal Tedder, Commanding Officer of RAF Middle East Air Command, urged a single unified air command over the whole of the Mediterranean as early as November 1942. In December General Eisenhower appointed General Carl Spaatz to

Left: *15th AF B-24s pick their way through flak over Blechhammer, Germany.*

Top: *One of the four Liberators attached to 108 Squadron.*

Bottom: *H.R.H. The Duke of Gloucester inspects 108 Squadron at Ismalia, Egypt, 7 June 1942.*

376th BG 'Liberandos' thread their way across the snow-capped Alps.

co-ordinate the operations of Eastern Air Command and the 12th AF but it was not until mid-January 1943, during the Casablanca Conference, that Tedder's original proposition was accepted. In the third week of February 1943 Mediterranean Air Command and North West African Air Forces, commanded by Spaatz and consisting of Eastern Air Command, 12th Air Force, and other units, were officially created.

Meanwhile 9th AF Liberators continued flying numerous missions in support of the Allied forces in Tunisia. By March 1943 Rommel's last offensive of the war had been repelled and by the summer, the two 9th AF Liberator Groups, the 376th and 98th, had been joined by three B-24 Groups from the 8th AF in England. As previously described in the Ploesti Chapter their task was the bombing of the Rumanian oilfields. In the run-up to the raid the 8th AF Liberators bombed targets in Italy. William Foulkes, who was now based at Tukrch on the Libyan coast a few miles north of Benghazi, saw them pass over on that fateful morning of Sunday, 1 August: 'We thought it odd because it was a large force by Middle East standards but of course were not aware they were heading for Ploesti at the time. The return was terrible. There was nothing we could do but watch in horror as they flew over, just a few hundred feet in the air, struggling, some with holes in their fuselages. Some were on three engines; others even on two.'

The survivors made another long-distance raid to the Wiener Neustadt aircraft factory in Austria before the three 8th AF Groups returned to England and the 98th 'Pyramiders' and the 376th 'Liberandos' were transferred to the 12th AF.

In October 1943 General Henry H. Arnold proposed a plan to split the American 12th AF in two to create a Strategic Air Force, leaving the remaining half of the 12th as a tactical organization. The possibility of a Strategic Air Force based in southern Italy would enable the Allies more easily to strike at targets like Ploesti and the aircraft factories at Wiener Neustadt. It would also complement the vast aerial armadas already operating from England. The enemy would be hard pressed to meet this second threat which would effectively put parts of Germany and eastern Europe, previously out of range of the 8th AF, within easy reach. Italy also had considerably better weather conditions than Britain. Arnold's plan was accepted and on 1 November 1943 the 15th AF was officially established. Initially the 376th, 98th and four B-17 groups formed the operational element of the 15th AF, based in the Foggia area. New groups soon started arriving from the United States, most of which were equipped with B-24s. Between December 1943 and May 1944 thirteen new Liberator groups joined the 15th AF.

Between 1 October 1943, when Liberators made their first attack from Foggia on the aircraft factories of Wiener Neustadt, and 8 May 1945 the 15th AF blasted a wide range of targets throughout Germany and the Occupied countries. Cities in southern Germany were raided and even targets as far away as Budapest and Pecs in Hungary and Czechowicka in Poland were bombed by 15th AF 'heavies'. Towards the end of the war, 15th AF Liberators and Fortresses attacked targets in France in support of Operation Anvil. Marseille, Lyon, Grenoble, and Toulon all felt the weight of their bombs.

Less publicized are the achievements of the Liberators of No. 205 Group of the Royal Air Force in the Mediterranean. They not only flew daylight missions in their B-24s but night missions as well. The Group started as No. 257 Wing in the Egyptian Canal Zone, equipped with long-range bombers, mostly Wellingtons. In September 1941 it was re-designated 205 Group and attempts were made to reinforce the Wellington squadrons with other aircraft.

There were no suitable heavy night-bombers to be spared for 205 Group so it was decided to equip them with the Liberator, despite the fact that the B-24 had many operational disadvantages for night work, the principal one being the bright flames and white-hot turbo-supercharger exhausts which made the aircraft a beacon in the sky for night fighters. Since night-fighter activity was not as intense over Italy and southern Europe as it was in the north-west it was considered that losses from night fighters would not be high. A further disadvantage was the 0.50 calibre machine-guns which had a much better range than the 0.303 guns but as the gunner could not see far enough in the dark to avail himself of this, the only advantage was their superior hitting power. However, it was found that as soon as the gunner fired, the flash from the guns ruined his night vision so he had little chance of aiming on a second attack. The front gun turret was also useless, as was the under gun turret as the light from the turbo-chargers made it impossible to see fighters at night.

So the RAF removed the under gun turret and the guns from the front turret, which was then faired over with fabric. The beam guns were also taken out because it was found that fighter attacks always came from behind. However, conversion to the Liberator was slow. On 15 January 1943 No. 178 Squadron was formed at Shandur in the Suez Canal Zone from a detachment of 160 Squadron and began receiving Liberator Mark IIIs. The following night three Liberators took off and bombed targets in Tripoli. It was not a full-scale beginning and 178 remained the only Liberator Squadron in 205 Group until October 1944, although on 14 March 1943 a 'Special Liberator' Flight was formed at Gambut, Libya. It was later re-designated 148 Squadron and began special duties, dropping arms and supplies to Resistance groups in Albania, Greece, and Yugoslavia.

In January 1944 148 Squadron moved to Italy and when not engaged in special operations its aircraft joined with other squadrons of 205 Group on heavy bombing raids on northern Italy and southern Europe. By April 1944, the powerful Mediterranean Allied Strategic Force was playing a vital role in the conduct of the war which was by no means confined to Italy or the Italian Front. The 15th AF continued to pound targets by day while the RAF Liberators and Wellingtons struck under the cover of darkness. By June the combined forces bombed railway networks in south-east Europe in support of Russian military operations in Rumania. Throughout the summer of 1944 Austrian aircraft manufacturing centres at Wiener Neustadt were bombed day and night and oil-producing centres, too, were bombed, often in conjunction with Bomber Command in England. By the autumn of 1944 these attacks had assumed top priority. Vast aerial fleets of 15th AF Liberators and B-17s escorted by Mustangs and Lightnings, attacked the refineries at Ploesti and bombed Budapest, Komarom, Gyor, and Petfurdo in Hungary, Belgrade and other cities in Yugoslavia and Trieste in north-eastern Italy. Meanwhile, Liberators and Wellingtons of No. 205 Group flew unescorted at night from their bases in southern Italy and stoked up the fires left by the American bombers.

Of special importance to the Germans were the Hungarian and Rumanian railway systems. These came under constant Allied aerial bombardment and in the summer of 1944 the Germans were deprived of the use of the Lwow-Cernauti Railway by the Russians. The only alternative route linking Germany with the grainlands of Hungary and the oilfields of Rumania was the River Danube, capable of

carrying 10,000 tons of war material daily. It was estimated that eight million tons of material had reached Germany in 1942 by this waterway alone. By mid-March 1944 the Danube was carrying more than double the amount carried by rail. Even a temporary halt in this river traffic would seriously hamper the German war effort and in April 1944 No. 205 Group began 'Gardening' operations, 'sowing' the waterways with mines. On the night of 8 April three Liberators and nineteen Wellingtons from 178 Squadron dropped forty mines near Belgrade. Over the next nine days 137 more mines were dropped and in May the total number dropped had risen to over 500. No 'Gardening' sorties were flown during June but on the night of 1 July sixteen Liberators and fifty-three Wellingtons dropped 192 mines in the biggest operation of the mining campaign. The following night another sixty mines were dropped.

At first the 'Gardening' sorties were only flown on nights of the full moon as the aircraft had to fly no higher than 200 feet and even heights of forty and fifty feet were reported. 'Gardening' sorties continued throughout July, August, and September. On the night of 4 October four Liberators and eighteen

Its tail knocked off by flak, a B-24 of the 15th AF plunges to earth during a raid on Blechhammer.

Wellingtons flew the final mission of the operation and dropped fifty-eight mines in the Danube in Hungary west of Budapest, north of Gyor, and east of Esztergom. In six months of operations, 1,382 mines were laid by Liberators and Wellingtons of No. 205 Group in eighteen attacks.

The effect on the supply route was catastrophic. Several ships were sunk and blocked the waterway in parts and by May coal traffic had virtually ceased. Canals and ports were choked with barges and by August 1944 the volume of material transported along the Danube had been reduced by about 70 per cent.

Meanwhile yet another Air Command had come into existence in the Mediterranean theatre—the Balkan Air Force. Its formation in June 1944 was a logical step in the sequence of events which had begun in April 1941 when Yugoslavia had been invaded by the Germans. Various Partisan groups became a constant menace to the occupying troops and in February 1944 the British Prime Minister, Winston Churchill announced that no less than

fourteen of the twenty German divisions as well as six other satellite divisions were being contained in the Balkan Peninsula, by a force of 250,000 Yugoslav Partisans supplied by elements of the RAF and American air forces in the Mediterranean.

Four Liberators from No. 148 Squadron had been supplying Resistance groups in Albania, Greece, and Yugoslavia since May 1942. In March 1943 Halifaxes became available and this squadron provided the nucleus of a Special Operations Air Force, which by June 1944 consisted of eight squadrons, including one flight of Liberators, and was manned by personnel from no less than five nations. This arrangement was nothing new. The officers and men of the 376th Bomb Group of the 15th AF was operated from October 1943 by Yugoslav nationals trained in the United States. They made their operational début in November 1943 in four B-24J Liberators presented to them by President Roosevelt at Bolling Field upon completion of their training. On 16 November the Yugoslavs joined with the 376th crews in

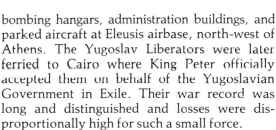

Left: *Losses on the early low-level Ploesti missions resulted in the 15th AF using high altitude bombing techniques against the Rumanian refineries.*

Above: *Liberator Mark VI of the Balkan Air Force.*

bombing hangars, administration buildings, and parked aircraft at Eleusis airbase, north-west of Athens. The Yugoslav Liberators were later ferried to Cairo where King Peter officially accepted them on behalf of the Yugoslavian Government in Exile. Their war record was long and distinguished and losses were disproportionally high for such a small force.

Special Operations Executive (SOE) units also operated from the Mediterranean during the war. By May 1943 many flights had been made to Poland from England. Between August and October 1943 brief use was made of three Liberators (BZ 859, 860, and 362, later transferred to 1586 Flight) but these long trips were subject to heavy fighter opposition and the risks were great. It was decided, therefore, to operate SOE aircraft from the Mediterranean theatre. No. 1575 Flight (which became 624 Squadron in 1943), No. 1586 Flight (which became 301 (Pomeranian-Polish) Squadron in November 1944), and 148 Squadron were based at Blida, Derna, and Tocra in North Africa, although airfields in Italy were used on occasions

in 1944, principally Brindisi but also Foggia. G. J. Hill, a fitter with 148 Squadron at Brindisi in August 1944, recalls the Polish Liberators: 'We used these Polish Liberators to convert some of the crews on to B-24s. Our Commanding Officer, Squadron Leader Dickie Knight and his flight engineer, had served on Liberators before so they were given the job of converting the rest of the crews. After a very short time we received a batch of B-24Js from a maintenance unit in Algiers. The old Polish Liberators were flown back by the crews who had ferried in the new B-24s.'

Liberators, Lysanders, and Halifaxes based in southern Italy ranged throughout the Balkan countries, Czechoslovakia, southern France and, towards the end of the war, Austria and Germany, dropping 'Joes', Resistance leaders, arms, and supplies. By the end of the war the Balkan Air Force had flown over 11,500 sorties into Yugoslavia and had delivered over 16,400 gross tons of supplies to the Partisans. On the personnel side, 2,500 persons had been flown in and 19,000 brought out of the country.

Although the Balkans was the centre of operations for the special force, in August 1944 another supply mission was required farther north. The Russian armies had swept aside German resistance in Poland and were at the approaches of Warsaw. The Polish Home Army under General Bor was persuaded to rise against the German occupation troops but the Russians made no attempt whatever to support the rising. On the eve of 1 August 1944 General Bor requested all possible air support for the rising but for some time the Russians refused to allow RAF and American aircraft, involved in supplying arms to Warsaw, to make emergency landings in Russian-held territory. Bor pleaded for the bombing of the environs of the capital, the dispatch of Polish fighter squadrons from France, and even the dropping of the Polish parachute brigade into Warsaw itself. His pleas were, however, impractical. His fourth demand, that of increasing the air supply of arms and ammunition was just possible, involving as it did, a round trip of about 1,750 miles. Much of the journey would be over enemy-held territory bristling with anti-aircraft defences and night fighters.

The Special Duty squadrons in England were fully committed to 'Overlord' so the task of supplying the Polish Home Army was given to the Mediterranean Allied Air Forces. At first

Centre: *A tight-knit formation of 15th AF Liberators en-route to Wiener-Neustadt, twenty-seven miles south of Vienna.*

Right Top: *A 376th BG Liberator falls victim to a flak shell during a raid on Toulon, France.*

Right Centre: *Extra Joker of the 451st BG, 15th AF, has its fuel tanks ruptured by FW-190s shortly before bombing the Focke-Wulf factory at Markersdorf on 20 August 1944.*

Right Bottom: *Bombs tumble from the bays of a 465th BG Liberator hit in the fuel tanks by flak during a bomb-run over Blechhammer, Germany.*

Air Marshal Slessor opposed the plan on the grounds that the undertaking was suicidal but after appeals to Russia had failed and the Polish situation became more acute he was forced to agree to a small trial sortie being dispatched from No. 1586 (Polish) Special Duty Flight. These few aircraft proved successful and two Liberator Squadrons, No. 31 (SAAF) and No. 178 of 205 Group, were diverted from the invasion of southern France to support them. But Slessor's worst fears were realized and on the five nights between the 12 and 17 August, seventeen of the ninety-three aircraft despatched failed to return. The South Africans, were hit badly, losing eight Liberators in four nights.

With that operations ceased but were restarted after protests from the Polish authorities with aircraft from No. 1586 Flight. Four of the nine aircraft failed to return on two nights and after further losses bad weather prevented any further missions to the beleagured Poles. In early September the Russians finally agreed to co-operate but by then the Polish, RAF, and SAAF units had lost thirty-one aircraft out of 181 dispatched in twenty-two nights of operations.

Meanwhile the Liberators of the 15th Air Force and No. 178 Squadron continued pounding enemy targets throughout the Mediterranean and its immediate area. No. 178 Squadron had been using Liberators since the beginning of 1943 and had built up an impressive record, listing among its targets those of Crete, the Aegean Islands, and the Ploesti oil refinery. Apart from a few scattered units employing a handful of Liberators, up to October 1944, 178 was the only true RAF B-24 squadron in the Mediterranean. But that month 37 Squadron, based at Tortorella, began exchanging its Wellingtons for the Liberator Mark VI. During the year this Squadron had flown many operations not only dropping Partisans and mining the Danube, but also normal bombing raids.

As more and more Liberators became available, three more Wellington squadrons converted to Liberators in the first three months of 1945. In January that year 70 Squadron at Tortorella began re-equipping with Liberator VIs, as did 104 Squadron at Foggia Main, a month later. In March 1945, 40 Squadron also began converting to Liberator VIs at Foggia Main.

Crews were doubtless pleased with their new breed of bomber, which was different in every way from the Wellington and most other aircraft. Although it did not have the standard British blind flying panel which contained all the vital flying instruments—the instruments were arranged somewhat haphazardly and checks for take-off and landing were only possible by having the flight engineer read out from a long check list—it did have a superb radio and auto-pilot. The auxiliary engine-driven generator (for use on ground to ensure enough electricity for hydraulic brake pressures etc.) removed the constant anxiety of losing brake power when taxi-ing, which had been experienced with the Wellington, due to the slow running engines not being able to maintain pressure. Pilots found the flight deck a dream. There was more room than in the 'Wimpey' and there was even a carpet on the floor. (The ashtrays were removed on delivery as no smoking was permitted in any British service aircraft.) In its flying handling the Liberator was a lumbering aircraft—'like flying a bus' but crews rapidly got used to its performance and even enjoyed its superior stability (and hence comfort). The tricycle undercarriage (which no British aircraft had at the time) was also vastly superior to tail-wheel designs both for visibility and ease of handling.

No. 205 Group could now call upon six Liberator bomber squadrons including two SAAF Squadrons. The SAAF Squadrons had played a large part in the Mediterranean war, dropping supplies to guerrillas and taking part in the mining operations in the Danube. Not all the personnel in the South African squadrons were natives of that country. Quite often replacements were RAF personnel trained in Egypt and Palestine like Frank Mortimer, a Liberator air-gunner who was one of those who joined 34 Squadron (SAAF) in October 1944. He recalls: 'We arrived at Foggia and reported to 34 SAAF at Tortorella. Our living accommodation was four to a tent. It was raining at the time and ours was on a slope. There were no beds. I was fortunate to have a sleeping-bag with me. All around the airfield, which had been a maintenance unit for the Germans, were

wrecked Junkers 88s. None of the JU-88s had tyres. They had been stolen by the Italians to mend their plimsolls. I took a rudder off a JU-88 and slept on that for a few weeks. We also made radio sets from parts of their wreckage which we finished off with bent pins and razor blades, using our aircraft headsets for earphones.

'There was no place to dry out flying clothes so we slept in them. The dampness was intense and on raids we flew in wet clothes. The dampness also got into the parachutes and it is doubtful whether they would have worked when needed. We tried to make the tents more habitable by digging down about four feet to make more headroom. We also stole runway sheeting and used that to prop up the sides. Cleaning was another problem. There was a bowser which brought one jerry can of water every day. In Foggie we used to try and take a bath but it was over-populated with Americans and the British Army. Gradually as crews were shot down it was the custom to raid their tents, and take little luxuries, like a wooden bed. It was dog eat dog, with little sentiment at all.

'Our first two operations were supply drops to Tito's Partisans in Yugoslavia. These were completed under code names, flying about 100 feet over the DZs. I recall very vividly flying in the region of 500 feet. We dropped sugar, boots, rifles and other supplies and we could quite clearly see horses and carts coming to pick them up. During briefing for a raid on Yugoslavia we were told that there were three main Partisan groups involved—Tito, Mihailovich's men, and the Chetniks. We were told to watch out for the Chetniks because they were known to help the Germans look for downed airmen.

Top: Little Queen II *a Mark VI of No. 2 (SAAF) Wing. Both 31 and 34 Squadrons (SAAF) were equipped with the B-24 and operated from Italy with as part of 205 Group. In August 1944 31 Squadron lost eight B-24s in four nights during supply drops to the beleagured Polish Home Army in Warsaw and in six weeks the squadrons had lost twenty-four of their thirty-three aircraft.*

Centre: *Not a scene from the First World War but RAF living conditions at Foggia.*

Bottom: *The B-24D The Blue Streak of the 376th BG passes Mount Vesuvius. In the summer of 1945 an RAF Liberator from 178 Squadron crashed into the volcano and remains there to this day.*

'Most of the RAF crews were posted to 70 (ATF) Squadron in January 1945 and the SAs gave us a farewell party. I for one was proud to have flown with them. They were good men and I'll always remember the CO; he was a fantastic man. No. 70 Squadron's base was no better. The Sergeants' Mess was another cowshed and the food was foul. I lived off tins of South African pears and peaches. The place was infested with snakes and I even saw a warrant officer cutting one up to make a tie out of it.'

In January 1945 Denis Allen joined No. 40 Squadron at Foggia Main from 1675 HCU at Abu-Suier in the Canal Zone: 'I was delayed by the smallpox epidemic in Cairo and arrived on the Squadron a few days after my first crew (Skipper F/S Smout), only to find they had gone on their first op without me, and failed to return.

'I became acquainted with many US aircrew, both at Foggia and at Prestwick, where I did the automatic pilot course. I remember with great affection these quiet, serious young men with their easy-going temperament and good nature. The Commanding Officer of 40 Squadron, Group Captain Smythe, placed me with Pilot Officer Colin Dunn's crew who had lost their flight engineer. PO Dunn and crew had already completed ten 'ops' and despite the natural reluctance of all crews to take on a 'rookie' like myself, they made me welcome and I always considered myself lucky to join such a friendly and experienced crew. I flew eight 'ops' with my new crew, including one daylight mission. Our daylight 'op' was interesting—the target, a wharf named Arsa, was too small to bomb at night. We went in just above the altitude for accurate flak at about 24,000 feet. This was too high for such a small target so we were instructed to drop one bomb as a marker, make the necessary corrections on the bomb sight and go round again and drop the rest of the bomb load. On approaching the target we were immediately subjected to deadly-accurate flak and after a brief discussion with our bomb-aimer we decided to use the marker-bombs dropped by two Libs who were ahead of us. The bomb-run was very 'dicey'. When the bomb-doors were closed, full power was applied and a steep climbing turn executed. My hands were shaking so violently that I couldn't make my log entry for several minutes.'

Having so many groups in such a confined area caused many problems, as Frank Mortimer recalls: 'Foggia Plain comprised four airfields very close to each other. The flight paths overlapped and the risk of collision was very high. On one occasion two Liberators collided and we had to take the corpses to Bari cemetery. We collected them from the hospital in Foggia which was piled up with coffins. While going through the dock area an ammunition ship exploded and within minutes we were surrounded by hundreds of running Italians.

'As a result of the collision an order was made stating that the rear gunner had to remain in his turret to look out and warn of collision. Inside the tail turret was a notice which said OWING TO HIGH ACCELERATION GUNNERS MUST NOT LAND WHILE IN THE TURRET: The first time I actually landed in the turret it was a daylight raid. We had been warned to brace ourselves because the tail unit shook terrifically on a tricycle under-carriage but fortunately it was a very smooth landing. An aircraft rarely lands straight, it lands sideways, and this causes a lot of acceleration. The second time I landed in the turret was after a night raid and I suppose I was a bit cocky and didn't brace myself. I remember that I banged my head on the gunsights.

'The other dangerous practice was dropping the photoflash to enable us to make a photo-record of the bombing. It was a very dangerous 'pyro' in a long cylinder about three foot long, and usually dropped at the same time the bomb-aimer called "bombs away".

'It was well known that many photo flashes had hung up in the bomb-bay and blown the aircraft in two. Our pilot was very wary of them and asked the rear gunner to throw it out of the rear turret during bombs away. The flash had two safety devices on it. Two wires like hooks on a fishing line connected the fuse to two lines clipped on to the side of the fuselage. It was my job to see that the two fuses came out as the 'pyro' descended. It was a very 'Heath Robinson' affair and extremely frightening. Prior to throwing out the photo-flash we had to jettison large bundles of leaflets out of the window.

'The rear turret was fitted out for electrical flying-suits although we didn't get these until the end of the war. Owing to dampness in the tents we got a lot of shorting out. On one raid my gloves caught fire and I had to throw them out of the turret. After that I used only silk gloves. My main clothing was two pairs of silk underpants, two vests, probably a shirt and RAF pullover, plus an inner suit. There was no way I could wear an Irvine jacket in the cramped confines of the turret.'

By early 1945 the war seemed to get more vicious rather than the reverse. During a briefing RAF Liberator crews learned that one airman who had baled out had been hanged on the nearest lamp-post by Italian fascists. RAF Liberator crews were still coming through to replace those lost on operations although their training was not as complete as it could have been. Deryck Fereday, a pilot who joined 178 Squadron in March 1945 recalls: 'Pilots for 178 Squadron were taken from those who had undergone the OTU (Operational Training Unit) on Wellingtons—several in Palestine. Then instead of going straight to a squadron at Foggia they went to 1675 HCU (Heavy Conversion Unit) at Abu Suair, Egypt. The OTU course was five weeks and HCU only three. I still cannot believe that in so short a

Top: *Both 205 Group (RAF) and the 15th AF bombed Ploesti throughout the war. Here, Liberators of the 449th BG start fires in the Astro Romano oil refinery complex.*

Centre: *W for William of 70 Squadron, 231 Wing, 205 Group (RAF), Foggia.*

Bottom: *Italy was originally selected for 15th AF operations due to its proximity to targets out of* *range of the 8th AF and because the weather was thought to be ideal. Generally this was so but heavy rainfall sometimes proved a big problem on the improvized airfields.*

Centre Top: *P-38
Lightnings buzz 614
Squadron Liberators at
dispersal on Foggia Plains.*

Centre Bottom: *A 614
Squadron Liberator comes
into land at Foggia with
B-17s of the 99th BG 15th
AF in the background.*

time I sufficiently mastered the intricacies of
such an advanced aircraft to be entrusted with
the lives of seven men and 8,000 lb of high
explosive, not to mention thirty tons of
Liberator. I joined 178 Squadron at Amendola
along the Manfredonia road from Foggia,
which we shared with 614 Pathfinder Squadron
—just converting from Wellingtons to
Liberators. The airfield had only one runway,
2,000 yards long (essential for a fully loaded
Liberator), constructed of perforated steel
planking laid straight on the ground. The
surface was far from level with plenty of
friction to retard acceleration on take-off. With
only one runway it meant that we could be as
much as ninety degrees out of wind which
presented severe flying problems.

'Operations were mainly to northern Italy,
Austria, and Yugoslavia, and nearly all the
raids, until towards the end of the war, were to
railway junctions. I did just two daylight raids,
both to coastal targets. It would have been
suicide to have tried to go inland with our
depleted fire-power but a hit-and-run raid
could be pulled off.

'A typical raid took about five hours, usually
taking off at 22.00 or 23.00 hours and returning
in the small hours of the morning. For a
maximum effort the Group could muster about
seventy aircraft. For a 'sustained effort' this was
cut back to about forty or fifty aircraft to
ensure enough carry-over of serviceable aircraft
to the next night. The Liberators had a much
better serviceability record than the Wimpeys,
which were truly clapped-out.

'So the bomber force was much fewer than in
operations from the UK. But we all had to be
over the target in a bombing cloud or 'stream'
within three minutes instead of the ten or fifteen
minutes usual in north-west Europe. This was
essential to prevent flak singling out individual
planes and meant that we had to navigate very
precisely indeed. The Liberator's wonderful
electrical and radio equipment, stability in
flying, and good auto-pilot, was a big help in
this direction. Incidentally, because the Air
Ministry supposed Italian-based Liberators met
less opposition than the heavy bombers based
in the UK, the tour of duty for crews was
increased from thirty to forty operations. The
chances of survival for crew members (and
planes) was therefore theoretically the same.

'The small towns on the railways through the
Alps were defended out of all proportion to
their size because of the vital German need to
keep their supply routes open. Towns like
Bruch and Villach in Austria, and Ljubljana in
Yugoslavia, were typical. Certainly there were
plenty of legitimate targets down there in the
dark. For example, I remember one such raid to
Pragersko, a tiny junction in Yugoslavia, where
we obviously hit a munitions supply train as
the explosions on the ground were like a
firework display and even at 15,000 feet we had
the feeling of flying right through an inferno.

'Most raids were flown at around 12,000 to
15,000 feet. There was no point in going higher
and losing accuracy in bombing. Over the
target we had to stagger our bombing heights to
lessen the chance of collisions and sometimes
we had to descend to say 8,000 feet, if we had
been allocated one of the lower levels. This
meant that instead of being able to get the hell
away from the target, flak, and prowling night
fighters, we had to climb at slower speed to get
back to bomber-stream height. Also on raids to
Austrian targets, we had to get back over the
Alps.

'On 23 March 1945, after bombing a rail
junction and marshalling yard near Innsbruck,
we had to climb immediately in order to clear

Above: *Bombs dropped by a 70 Squadron Liberator cascade on to V for Victor of 37 Squadron during a raid on the shipyards at Manfalcone, Italy on 16 March 1945. Although the bombs had not fallen far enough to become 'live' the perspex in Wally Lewis's mid-upper turret and the port inner propeller were both ripped away, leaving a large hole in the fuselage behind Squadron-Leader L. Saxby, the pilot, and hitting Flight Sergeant Cliff Hurst, the WOP, in the back, leaving him unconscious. However, V for Victor limped home to Tortorella, more than 300 miles away and landed safely. Squadron Leader Saxby and his bomb-aimer, P/O G. T. Barker can be seen inspecting the damage.*

the mountains. Had we been only slightly off course we could not have made it, due to the higher peaks on either side. This night we entered cloud as we turned from the target for home. The cloud was coloured red from the ground fires and there was no visual contact with the mountain peaks all around. As we climbed the Liberator seemed slower than usual and we seemed to be heading directly for a mountain. I turned the electronic boost control into 'Emergency position 10' and the Lib seemed just to jump upwards. At that moment we broke cloud into a magnificent scene of the Tyrolean Alps in bright moonlight. Fortunately we were safe at the necessary height so I was able to reduce boost and avoid further overstressing the engine. The panorama below was breathtakingly beautiful and a strong contrast to the scene of death and destruction we had just created only a few miles away.

'Towards the end of the war a new type of operation was introduced. Instead of strategic bombing we switched to close support for the 8th Army's final offensive of the war as the front moved into the plains of the Po valley. We were 'blanket bombing' the German troop positions just before the 8th Army launched a local attack, sometimes going for a small bridge area or a bottleneck as part of the total operation. There was no identifiable bombing point that we could find on our own so we had to bomb on Pathfinder markers which were dropped using dead reckoning or radar.

'There was no Gee, unlike in western Europe as we were out of range, which was a pity as it was the best navigational aid in existence and highly accurate. Instead we had 'Loran', which used stations 500 to 1,000 miles away and allowed no instant fixes, so as far as we could we used other methods. On these tactical raids we were in effect using the Liberators at night to reinforce what the American light bombers were doing in the daytime.'

Arthur Jeffries, a beam gunner with 40 Squadron, flew on the Po raid on the night of 18 April. He recalls: 'The briefing for the raid took a little longer than usual due to the complexities of this range of targets. Our own particular sector was at Malalburgo. We could hardly believe our ears when we were told that we were laying a barrage only a 1,000 yards ahead of the 5th Army—and at night! The time for take-off was at 19.25 hours.

'The Pathfinders (614 Squadron Liberators) were to drop markers, and our navigator and bomb-aimer would be further assisted by members of the ground units firing tracer shells at the enemy positions. Timing was of prime importance. We arrived in *E for Easy* a couple of minutes early and had to resort to a navigational trick or two to rectify this. Right on time the marker flares were dropped and the tracer shells indicated the target. From then on our bombing run began. Ted Hawes, our bomb-aimer, was in complete control, cool and confident. A quick look at our target area and we all knew that this 'first' night-support attack had been a success. Only light anti-aircraft fire was encountered and the night fighters were conspicuous in their absence. Letters of congratulation were received from General Alexander and General McCreery on the success of the mission.'

On 25 April 1945, 205 Group crews were briefed for an operation that was a return to rail junction and marshalling yard raids after their close support work. Sixty-one Liberators were dispatched to the marshalling yards at Freilassing in Austria about four miles north-west of Salzburg. No. 614 (County of Glamorgan) Squadron dispatched seven Pathfinder Liberators to illuminate and mark the yards. Deryck Fereday was among the bomber crews who took part: 'The operation took an hour longer than usual due to the greater distance (I logged six hours five minutes, carrying two 1,000 lb and ten 500 lb bombs). It went completely to the pattern of other raids: heavy flak over the target, lots of ground explosions and flames indicating munitions in the rail trucks destroyed. Coming back we climbed with plenty of time before we reached the Alps so I permitted myself the luxury of 'listening out' on the pilot's standard frequency radio, which was controlled from above the pilot's head in the roof of the flight deck and could be tuned to almost any broadcast frequency (normally we used only the push button VHF radio for ground/air control, plus the WOP's Morse set). Loud and clear was an Austrian station playing Strauss waltzes, without commentary or other introduction, just showing that someone down there was determined to end the war in three-four time. Even today hearing the 'Blue Danube' brings on instant Liberator nostalgia.

'This was the last bombing raid of the war. We stood by for other operations but none

were confirmed: indeed the fighting lines were so fluid that no one quite knew what point the invading armies had reached. Then VI— Victory in Italy Day—was announced on 6 May 1945. We won the war in Italy with the help of the Liberator, two days before VE-Day was announced in the West.'

During 1945 Liberators flew British troops from Italy to Athens to help suppress the ELAS rising. This caused unrest among South African crews because many were of Greek extraction. On the very last day of the war and for a few days after the German surrender in Italy, Liberators transported petrol and supplies to the British 8th Army advancing from northern Italy into Austria.

Denis Allen of 40 Squadron recalls: 'During the summer of 1945 we made several flights to northern Italy carrying petrol and army rations. These flights were regarded as an 'easy' number but in fact proved just as hazardous as a 'normal' mission! The trouble arose from the temporary landing strip. The Liberator soon broke-up the sun-baked turf and produced large areas of soft sandy soil which hindered take-off. On one occasion I remember even with 120 on the clock the Liberator simply refused to leave the runway.'

No. 148 Squadron was also involved with 'trooping' duties as G. J. Hill recalls: 'We were given the job of transporting POWs back to the UK as part of Operation Exodus. Benches were fitted and bomb-doors were sealed with doped fabric to keep the draughts out. However, a steady slipstream blew through the holes and the fuselage was below freezing for most of the trip. We carried twenty-seven passengers at a time in the bomb-bays and during the flight, we let them up into the back of the Liberator for a smoke, one at a time—the poor Bs! The passengers could see nothing and there was no method of communicating with them other than by shouting to the first man and asking him to pass it on.'

One by one the Liberator squadrons left Italy. On 6 November 1945 148 Squadron left Foggia and flew to Gianacalis in Egypt. G. J. Hill remembers the trip: 'We carried everything we could get on these aircraft and we took possibly the only two pigs to fly on Liberators. The pigs had been with 148 a long time and were well fed with the swill from three messes. It was a sight to behold to see pigs' heads looking out of large beam windows as the Lib took off from Foggia. On 25 January 1946 148 Squadron was disbanded at Gianacalis. We had a wonderful farewell party—and we ate our two pigs!'

On 13 November 178 Squadron moved to Fayid, Egypt, and towards the end of December was disbanded. Crews were posted to 70 Squadron of 205 Group at Shallufa, Egypt. Trooping continued until in February 1946 crews heard that they were to change to Lancs flown by new crews who would be coming out

from the UK. The Libs were to be given back to the Americans, as Britain saw no point in paying for them when ample British aircraft were now available for bomber squadrons.

Deryck Fereday recalls: 'We ferried the Libs one by one to Gebel Hamzi (formerly known as 'Kilo 40') on the desert road from Cairo to Alexandria and El Alamein. The last trip was made on 20 March 1946 and we had to suffer the indignity of being brought back by a Lancaster crew whose knees were still white and who had never seen a shot fired in anger. The Libs at Gebel Hamzi were parked in two long lines stretching to the desert horizon. The Maintenance Unit closed down in September 1946 but not before German POWs were brought in to chop through the aircraft, breaking the tail-plane off, and hammering a spike sledge through each engine.

'By the time our last trip was made the first Libs had the sand washing over their tyres and had already been stripped by locals of anything saleable or of scrap value. It was a sorry sight, those beautiful and efficient flying machines in their graveyard, but they had done their job. It was the end of an era.'

The Forgotten Air Force

When Britain declared war on Germany in September 1939 urgent operational requirements in other theatres of war made it impossible to reinforce or modernize the pre-war air force in India. Until Japan's involvement in the war in December 1941 the Royal Navy had protected India's 3,000 mile coastline and her armies had defended her land frontiers and maintained internal stability. As a result, when Air Chief Marshal Sir Richard Peirse arrived in India at the beginning of March 1942 he discovered the RAF had no more than four squadrons. The most modern aircraft were a handful of Curtis Mohawks and three Indian Air Force squadrons equipped with obsolete

Hawker Hart biplane fighters and a few Lysanders.

In Burma the four fighter, three bomber and two Army Co-operation squadrons lacked the necessary repair and maintenance facilities and the only early warning system was maintained from inadequate observer posts. Early Japanese advances overwhelmed both air and ground forces and the sadly depleted squadrons were forced to retreat with the 14th Army to the Indian hinterland.

As the war progressed British material and personnel were reserved mainly for the Home front and the 14th Army sardonically named itself 'The Forgotten Army'. The Air Force

squadrons which supported and supplied it might justly have been called the 'Forgotten Air Force' as they too seemed always at the end of any list of priorities. Fortunately no further Japanese attacks were launched on India or Ceylon before the 1942 Monsoon giving the Allies the opportunity of building up their depleted squadrons.

In January 1942, 159 and 160 Squadrons reformed at Molesworth and Thurleigh respectively and were equipped with Liberator Mark IIs. At the end of January 1942 159 Squadron's ground personnel embarked for the Far East. Its Liberators flew out via the Middle East in June but became involved in long range bombing raids from Palestine and Egypt until September.

No 160 Squadron was given training on Liberators by 86 Squadron, and then flew to Nutts Corner, Northern Ireland, in May 1942 for a short period of anti-submarine patrols with Coastal Command before flying on to the Middle East in June. Their passage to India was halted while five Liberators provided air cover for convoys desperately needed for the relief of Malta. This was followed by bombing raids on Tobruk and others targets in the Meditarranean

area. In January 1943 its personnel was combined with that of 159 Squadron, remaining in the Middle East, and became 178 Squadron.

On 15 January 1943 160 Squadron was re-organized in Ceylon as a Liberator general reconnaissance unit. For the rest of the war it operated under the auspices of Headquarters 222 Group and later Area Headquarters Ceylon. In addition to patrols and shipping escort duties 160 Squadron flew long-range photographic reconnaissance missions over Sumatra and the Nicobar Islands.

During the first two weeks of October 1942 the first 159 Squadron Liberator IIs flew to India touching down at Salbani. Operations over the first few months were all made at night and rarely extended to more than five aircraft and sometimes only two. RAF Liberator crews sought targets at Akyab Island, Maungdaw, Buthidaung, Schwebo and the Mandalay and Rangoon areas. Later operations extended as far as Bangkok involving an air time of twelve or more hours. Losses in general were not high compared to Europe. This was because the Japanese normally held their aircraft back from the forward airfields in Burma unless they were

No. 99 Squadron (Madras Presidency) Liberators and their ground crews bask in the Indian sun.

mounting a specific offensive. Also, a high proportion of the Liberator's flying time on operations was spent over the waters of the Bay of Bengal and thus safe from ground fire. On the other hand the chances of getting home or surviving from a crashed aircraft were slim as far as operations over Burma were concerned.

Crews numbered about seven men for night operations, including a first and second pilot. Later flight engineers were posted to the squadrons supposedly in place of the second pilot. However both the second pilot and flight engineer were carried in the Liberators. This proved very unpopular with the crews, especially in view of the long distances flown. Towards the end of the Japanese campaign, additional gunners were carried on daylight operations increasing the crew to anything up to ten and even eleven. Serviceability was quite good, magneto drops and oleo legs being the main exceptions. Most major servicing was carried out at the maintenance unit at Drigh Road, Karachi. Later Liberator models arrived from the United States with many minor items of equipment missing and flight crews had to improvise, as Ronald French, a fitter with 159 Squadron, recalls: 'We had little or no equipment and even had to make trestles and stands out of bamboo.' Another fitter with 159 Squadron, Flight Sergeant Stanley Burgess, recalls those early days in the Squadron: 'Morale was low at the time. There was no mail from home and we could not get any spares for the aircraft. Even so we managed to get about four out of six Liberators ready for operations to Ramree and Akyab. Later Wing Commander Blackburn took command of the squadron and injected new life. We received Mark VI Liberators and later Mark VIIs and started a gradual build-up of spares and a regular supply of beer. At times the squadron flew with American Liberators on operations. They could never understand how we managed to take off with such heavy loads of fuel and bombs.'

On 10 May 1943, 354 Squadron was formed at Drigh Road, Karachi. At first the Squadron was to operate in a general reconnaissance role carrying out long range photographic reconnaissance but owing to the vulnerability of the single Liberator to enemy fighters, already experienced by 160 Squadron, its role was changed to convoy escort and anti-submarine

duty in the Bay of Bengal. The first convoy escort was carried out on 4 October 1943 from Cuttack, where 354 assembled in August that year. By the time the Squadron moved to Minneriya, Ceylon, in October 1944, about 236 sorties had been carried out without the loss of a single ship from the convoys covered.

Another important part of the Squadron's role was the 'Maxim' anti-shipping patrols off the Arakan coast from the Mayu River to the mouth of the Irrawaddy. Liberators flew their first patrol on 11 December 1943 and continued daily without a single operational failure until 28 May 1944 when the monsoon prevented further operations. These patrols, which were of an average duration of twelve hours, were instrumental in preventing the Japanese from supplying their forces in the Arakan by means of large merchant vessels. Numerous small craft which the enemy was forced to use were sunk or damaged.

Allied offensive operations began in Burma in the spring of 1943. With the coming of the monsoon in June the Japanese practically ceased operations, withdrawing their units for training, rest, and re-equipment. Although the 14th Army failed in its objective to secure forward positions in the Arakan and hold them during the monsoon, air supremacy was maintained throughout the fighting and direct support was given to the troops. The small number of Liberators and Wellingtons available were afflicted with icing in the air and occasional cyclones on the ground. These storms were so fierce as to lift a Liberator at

dispersal bodily into the air. But Wellington and Liberator operations continued despite the appalling weather, disrupting the enemy's communications to such an extent that he was forced to move the bulk of his troops and supplies at night.

After the 1943 monsoon a re-organization of the Allied air forces was undertaken. On 18 August the Liberators in South East Asia were supplemented by the arrival of 355 Squadron, which was formed at Salbani, India. Its motto, 'Liberamus per caerula' (We liberate through tropical skies), could not have been more appropriate. The 355th flew its first mission of the war on the night of 19/20 November 1943, when three Liberators bombed the central railway station at Mandalay.

In November 1943, South East Asia Command, which had officially been created at the Quebec Conference, came into being and the following month British and American Air Forces in that theatre were combined to form a single operational whole. Air Chief Marshal Sir Richard Peirse was appointed Allied Air Commander-in-Chief under the direction of the Supreme Commander, Admiral Lord Louis Mountbatten. Responsibility for the prosecution of the air war against the Japanese from Eastern India was vested in the new Eastern Air Command with the American Major-General George E. Stratemeyer as Air Commander. The Command was staffed jointly by British and American officers and controlled all RAF and USAAF squadrons in Assam and Bengal.

Above: A 215 Squadron Liberator comes into land at an airfield in India. On New Year's Day 1945 a 215 Squadron Liberator piloted by Squadron Leader C. V. Beadon flew 1,000 miles back to base after being seriously damaged by flak and set on fire during a daylight raid on the Siam-Burma railway. The feat earned a command mention.

Below: A 7th BG Liberator passes over Bilin, Burma, after an attack on 13 November 1944. The 7th BG was the only American Liberator group in Burma and served with the Strategic Air Force.

Right: A neat formation of 99 Squadron Liberators over the Indian Ocean en route to their target.

Early in March 1944 the Japanese crossed the Chindwin River and advanced on Imphal. But by mid-June 1944 the Japanese had been routed, defeated by Lieutenant-General Slim's 14th Army, supported by SEAC squadrons of Liberators, Wellingtons, fighters, and transport aircraft. The shattered remnants of the Japanese army retreated across the Chindwin leaving behind 30,000 dead.

With the battles of Kohima and Imphal resolved the Allied High Command was able to resume its strategic offensive. The Americans wanted to open the road to China from Burma and mobilize the Chinese armies against the Japanese occupation forces. However, Slim wanted to force the Japanese to stand and fight in central Burma where he believed the 14th Army could destroy them. He was ultimately proved right and went on to take Rangoon, another of his objectives.

The British, Ghurka and Indian land forces were cheered by their victories but the hot steamy jungles and monsoon rains took their toll. The RAF and American 10th Air Force squadrons encountered similar problems. Just as the ground forces had to hack their way through the undergrowth, Indian coolies had to carve out improvised landing strips from the paddy fields in the Delta region. Although the runways were often of a high standard the construction of the dispersals left much to be desired. They should have been constructed with three layers of brick but the Indians were usually satisfied with just mud and as a result crews arrived in the early morning to find most of their Liberators completely bogged down.

But when the weather held and the dispersals were baked dry the Liberators took off from the RSP matting runways to seek their shipping targets in the warm waters of the Indian Ocean. The Allies had intercepted the Japanese codes and the British 'Y' service was responsible for passing on the intercepted information to the SEAC squadrons. Reports filtered through confirming the exact location of the Japanese ships and the Liberators sank them, almost at will. Meanwhile 'Earthquake' or 'Major' operations, were flown involving ten to twelve squadrons of RAF and American aircraft in support of General Slim's armies in the jungle offensive.

On 27 July 1944 356 Squadron flew its first bombing raid of the war. Seven Liberators were dispatched to bomb Yeu but one accidentally released all its bombs on the run-up to the target and the other six did not bomb because of cloud. Instead they flew on to Kongyi, accompanied by the Liberator without bombs, and hit an enemy supply dump.

By mid-1944 the Liberator was fast becoming one of the finest aircraft available for Burmese operations. One drawback had been the relatively small bomb load the Liberators could carry over the vast distances to their target. On operations involving distances of between 1,000 and 1,100 miles the maximum bomb load was considered to be only 3,000 lb. But Wing Commander J. Blackburn, Commanding Officer of 159 Squadron from July to December 1944, experimented with fuel consumption and soon increased the bomb load to 8,000 lb. The improvement was commended by the Americans and soon the example was followed by units throughout the Strategic Air Force. Eventually, round trips to targets as distant as the Kra Isthmus (2,300 miles), the Malay Peninsula (2,800 miles), and the approaches to Penang harbour (3,000 miles) were made carrying vastly increased bomb loads.

The news spread and in August 1944, 215 Squadron at Jessore, India, began converting from Wellingtons to Liberators. In September that year 99 Squadron, which was in the process of moving from Jessore to Digri, India and which had been operating against the Japanese since November 1942, also began replacing its ageing two-engined Wellingtons with Liberators. Its long-overdue conversion (the Squadron had been flying Wellington aircraft since October 1938) meant that it could now strike at targets in Thailand and Malaya.

In October 1944, 354 Squadron flew to Minneriya, Ceylon to take up anti-submarine patrols in the shark-infested waters of the Bay of Bengal. Upon their arrival it was discovered that the facilities existing would not permit the employment of all the Squadron aircraft and one flight was subsequently dispatched to Kankesanturai. During their stay in Ceylon 354 Squadron flew fifty-seven anti-submarine patrols over the shipping lanes of the Bay of Bengal, losing two Liberators, by which time

submarine activity in the Indian Ocean had completely ceased. The Liberators had played a very important part in protecting the supply lines to the Burma front and driving the enemy submarines from the area.

The Japanese found they were not safe from attack even when they were vast distances from Liberator bases. On the night of 27 October 1944 fifteen Liberators from 159 Squadron at Digri flew a round trip of more than 3,000 miles to mine the approaches to Penang harbour. One of the crew members on this operation was John Hardeman, a rear-gunner on the Liberator *Z for Zebra*, flown by Warrant Officer Bartter.

'We flew with a skeleton crew which meant a reduction in gunners (I being the only gunner on board). Apart from the skipper we flew a wireless operator, a navigator and a bomb aimer only, to save weight. All armament, save my rear turret guns, were removed and so was the armour plate with every effort to make the Liberator as light as possible. The front bomb bays were filled with bomb-bay tanks while the remaining bomb-bays were filled with about half a dozen 'non-sweepable' bakelite mines.

'We took off from Digri the day before the actual operation and flew to an advance landing ground close to Calcutta. It was occupied by the Americans as evidenced by B-29s parked everywhere. We were going to take off at a vastly overloaded weight and this was the reason for flying to the advance landing strip which had a longer runway than Digri. After taking on a full fuel load we were in the region of five thousand pounds overweight. The Americans were naturally inquisitive but we were not allowed to tell even them where we were going. Wing Commander Blackburn, who earned the highest respect of all the crews in 159 Squadron, took off first. If, when he was airborne, a green Very was fired then it would be safe for the rest of us to take off. We had to get a maximum run without "going through the gate" and climb at a very gradual rate. The Squadron watched the Wing Commander take off with bated breath. Sighs of relief went up as he became airborne. He fired the green light and off we went.

'During take-off I was up front in the flight deck. A rear gunner's job was to take charge of the auxiliary power unit located directly underneath the flight deck. Fortunately, the take-off was just as usual. But the extreme range of our mission was such that we had to perform a climbing rate that was unbelievably economical; so much so that we hardly noticed the ascent. There was certainly no strain imposed on the aircraft and we got rid of our excess fuel as quickly as we could to save more weight. We climbed very, very, gradually until we reached something like 20,000 feet. Bartter immediately throttled back and just dipped the nose so that we had in effect, a descent rate, more or less equivalent to the climbing rate. We

A 355 Squadron Liberator, identified by its vertical rudder markings, en route to its target with the ball turret extended. Towards the end of the Burma campaign ball turrets were removed because Japanese fighters were rarely encountered.

The mining operation, flown entirely over water, was carried out copybook fashion with an exceptional degree of navigational skill. Wing Commander Blackburn had prepared the operation right down to the last detail, including laying on 'air sea rescue'—a half-submerged submarine—in the event that any Liberator got into difficulties! The following day a Royal Navy carrier-borne aircraft brought back photographic evidence of shipping scuttled in the Penang approaches confirming the Liberators' accuracy.

The success achieved by 159 Squadron led, on 26 November 1944, to a second mining operation by Wing Commander Blackburn's crews in the approaches to Penang. It was a carbon copy of the first except that this time the Japanese were expecting the Liberators and fired on them.

That same day 99 Squadron flew its first Liberator operation of the war when twelve aircraft bombed the railway station and marshalling yards at Pyininana, Burma.

Ron Davies, a ball-turret gunner with 99 Squadron, recalls some experiences flying on Liberator operations. 'Each operation lasted anything from six to sixteen hours. Sometimes we flew so low that Indians used to throw rocks at us because we upset their bullocks pulling their carts. On one occasion the nose cone was shattered when we sheared the top of a palm tree.'

Many of 99 Squadron's operations were against the Burma railway, the Liberators going in at low level after the POWs, who were being forced to build it, had dispersed. Railway bridges were frequent targets and often bombed from zero feet, as Ron Davies recalls:

'On 13 December 1944 we took off at 07.30 hours for the Kyaikkatha railway bridge. Flying in the ball turret at zero feet (as far as the altimeter was concerned) I had a good view from underneath, skimming the tree tops. We ran into a clearing, the railway station was ahead and the target just beyond. I could see the signs on the platform quite clearly. Then we were on to the bridge but we were a little early. Mud and debris were still in the air from the previous aircraft's bombs, there being two seconds' delay on the bombs to allow us to get clear. We dropped our bombs, and ended up with mud plastering the sighting window of the ball turret. On the way out, while still in formation, we met up with Japanese fighters, one of which was destroyed, and one damaged.'

Mine-laying operations were again undertaken on 29 December 1944 when Liberators of 159 Squadron laid mines in the river approaches to Rangoon. John Hardeman flew his twenty-fourth and final mission of the war that day when he was selected as rear gunner for one of the six Liberators which took part.

'I flew with Flight Lieutenant Hall in

reached about fifty feet and levelled off for the mine-laying operation. The mines had a very bad habit of breaking up if they were dropped from a very high altitude and if they were dropped too low they had a bad habit of bouncing rather after the style of the Dam-buster bombs!

'We arrived at Penang at night quite amazed with ourselves because no one had ever flown this far south before. It was quite obvious from the illumination of Georgetown and other villages on Penang Island that the Japanese were certainly not expecting visitors. Light-houses were clearly seen and we had no trouble in determining our target or our mining direction. There were no fighters or flak—nothing! It was complete and utter surprise. We carried out our mining operation as though it was a conventional exercise, using our prescribed compass bearing.

'Our homeward trip was a replica of the outward journey except that we were that much lighter, possibly climbing that little bit faster. We flew straight back to base and not the advance landing ground, where we were debriefed.'

Liberator *Y for Yoke*. Much to my chagrin I was selected to fly with what was a special crew for this operation which meant I was parted from my normal crew who now flew with Warrant Officer Sinclair. My skipper, Warrant Officer Bartter, had already completed his tour, having flown a 'blooding operation' before becoming operational. I protested about not being able to fly with my regular crew but the decision was final.

'It was a well-planned operation with a diversionary raid laid on at high altitude to soak up any fighter opposition. We six flew at low-level over the Golden Pagoda, which was our initial point for the mining operation. At timed intervals each Liberator dropped a string of mines almost on the Pagoda's doorstep, all the way along the river and almost up to Elephant Point at the river's mouth. We flew position number five in the dropping order. All six aircraft dropped their mines and headed straight out to sea for home.

'We completed our drop according to plan without meeting any opposition. It appeared to be a carbon copy of the first raid on Penang, except the lights of Rangoon were out. We were

also very surprised at the absence of flak. It immediately brought to my mind the possibility that night fighters were around. Hardly had I warned the rest of the crew when I spotted an aircraft astern and slightly high. Although the moon was shining it was a dark night and I was unable to identify it. I warned the pilot that an unidentified aircraft was flying in the seven o'clock high position. Then all hell let loose from the ground. At a predetermined time the Japanese had switched on every available searchlight and had opened up every damn gun they had in the place.

'An inferno erupted on what was a peaceful night. Right in the middle of it all I saw the aircraft again. It was not a night fighter but another Liberator and it had been hit. It caught fire, keeled over and went in with one big explosion. It was only on our return about 100 miles from base, when we broke radio silence and the call signs came through, that I realized I had witnessed the destruction of my crew with whom I had flown twenty-three operations. It was a very sad day and I broke the news to 'Bing' Bartter the day after, explaining that there was no hope of any survivors.'

The long reach: RAF Liberators followed up their land attack raids with sorties against Japanese shipping far out into the Bay of Bengal and the Indian Ocean. These three photos by 159 Squadron were taken in Satahib Bay on 1 and 15 June 1945.

103

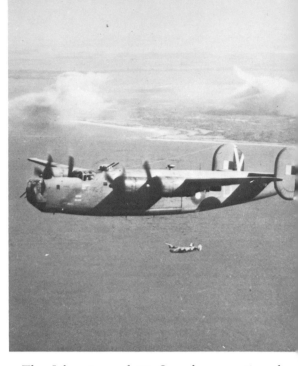

Above Left: *Three Liberators of 356 Squadron blast targets on Ramree Island. On Christmas Eve 1944 eight Liberators from the Squadron ventured further afield and bombed Hanoi at night.*

Above Right: *Liberator B Mark VIs of 356 Squadron hit Japanese positions on Ramree Island off the west coast of Burma just before the 8th Army landing in January 1945.*

Right Top: *Liberator B Mark VIs en route to Rangoon escorted by a lone RAF Thunderbolt.*

Right Centre: *500 lb bombs explode in Rangoon during a raid on the Burmese capital on 11 March 1945.*

Right Bottom: *Rangoon gaol was finally liberated on 1 May 1945. At first the Allies did not realize the Japanese had left. Prisoners tried to attract their attention by painting 'Japs Gone, Extract Digit' before they ran out of paint!*

No 159 Squadron's expertise in mine-laying operations continued and in January 1945 sixteen Liberators carried out a further mine-laying mission in the approaches to Penang.

On New Year's Day 1945, during a daylight raid on the Siam-Burma railway a Liberator B VIII, piloted by Squadron-Leader C. V. Beadon, was seriously damaged by flak and set on fire. Eventually, after three hours the fire was extinguished and the 1,000 mile flight home accomplished successfully. No. 215 Squadron flew many more very long-range operations over Burma before converting, in April 1945, to Dakotas.

Early in January 1945 354 Squadron returned to Cuttack to carry out anti-shipping operations in the Andaman Islands area off the southern Burmese and Tenasserin coasts. Numerous shipping lane patrols were flown to enable fuel consumption tests to be carried out. In February anti-shipping operations were resumed and during the month 354 flew eighteen sorties and five Japanese vessels were sunk. These attacks created a serious problem for the Japanese and with the continuous attacks by Eastern Air Command on the Burma-Siam railway the use of the sea route from Singapore to Rangoon became vital to the enemy.

The Allies had no such problem and new crews continued to arrive on the Liberator squadrons. Among them was Tom Henthorne who joined 99 Squadron as a co-pilot.

'My first operation was on 5 February when we bombed Japanese munitions hidden in the jungle at Madaya. There was no opposition but three days later when we hit Japanese concentrations at Yenanyaung we were met by intense flak. Our Liberator was slightly damaged. On 11 February the Squadron destroyed Japanese supply dumps at Rangoon without damage to the famous Shwe Dragon Pagoda near-by. There was a lot of flak but it didn't seem to worry the Japanese fighters, who attacked regardless. Three of them were shot down.'

The Liberators of 99 Squadron continued making sorties on supply dumps throughout the remainder of February, often leaving a pall of smoke over blazing Japanese fuel dumps. Flak was often light and 99 Squadron Liberators rarely encountered any fighter opposition. On 2 March the target they sought was the No. 1 railway yards at Bangkok. Tom Henthorne recalls: 'This was one of the few night sorties we made and it turned out to be very successful. The entire target area was left in a mass of flames. Only a few searchlights tried to find us but there was little flak and only one fighter, which got on our tail for a few seconds but soon veered off. Two days later we made a second night attack, this time on the Central railway yards at Bangkok. Later in the month, on 27 March, I returned to operations with a daylight sortie against Japanese supply dumps at Bangkok and two days later, against the Japanese Headquarters in Rangoon.'

By the end of March 1945 the decisive battle for central Burma had been won and Slim was eager to advance on Rangoon. At this point the Chinese and American forces were suddenly withdrawn. It proved a severe setback but was worsened by the unexpected decision to use the USAAF element of the air transport force to ferry the troops out. The entire mobility of the 14th Army depended on this force and the US Chiefs of Staff only relented after appeals from Admiral Lord Louis Mountbatten and Chiefs of Staff in London. The Americans put back the order for evacuation until 1 June or when Rangoon finally fell, whichever was the sooner.

The British chiefs need not have worried. Japanese reinforcements which tried to infiltrate from the west were checked by resistance groups and by a technique developed by Wingate's Chindits; clandestine ground observers with radio sets calling for air strikes by RAF Liberators. At the end of April cross-over patrols were flown by Liberators in the Andaman Sea to prevent a Japanese naval force

located at Singapore from interferring with Operation Dracula, the seaborne operations against Rangoon. But on 1 May, the day before the Dracula force was to land, a reconnaissance Mosquito flying over Rangoon saw painted on the roof of a gaol known to contain Allied POWs, the words 'Japs Gone. Extract Digit', which in RAF parlance meant 'pull your finger out!' Tom Henthorne was among those in 99 Squadron who successfully bombed coastal gun batteries that day unaware that the Japanese had pulled out.

On 2 May during an attack on Japanese gun positions in the Rangoon area, a Liberator from 355 ditched in the sea after an engine caught fire. Among those lost was the first RAF Fighter Command VC of the war, Wing Commander J. B. Nicolson, who was flying as an observer.

Meanwhile, valuable airmen who had served with Bomber Command in Europe began filtering through to RAF Liberator squadrons in the Far East. Leslie Parsons, a navigator and veteran of thirty-one operations on Lancasters in 1944, was one of the many posted to 1673 Heavy Conversion Unit, Kolar, near Bangalore, India, for training on Liberators. He joined 99 Squadron at Dhubalia near Krisnagar, about sixty miles north of Calcutta.

On 5 June 1945 99 Squadron attacked Japanese supply dumps and the railway at Suratthani (or Surasdhani) in the extreme south of Siam. Ron Davies, the ball-turret gunner on *G for George* was one of those who took off at 06.00 hours.

'Owing to the great distance the bomb load was reduced to 3,000 lb. The rest of the bomb-bay was filled with two 300 gallon overload tanks, which had to be pumped into the main wing tanks before the fuel could be used. There were two of us flying low at about 300 feet over the Bay of Bengal. (The Japs had a radar station at Rangoon and we hoped to avoid being picked up.) The other aircraft was about half a mile away on our beam, but for some reason was flying rather low. We sent messages on the Aldis lamp telling him to climb a little, as although the pilot was experienced over Germany, he was unused to the tropical, bumpy conditions, which could be experienced over the bay. He banked rather steeply without climbing. He dropped the wing tip, touched the sea, and the aircraft plunged straight under. With full tanks and bomb load it blew up instantly, the sea was on fire, and though we circled the spot for ten minutes, no sign could be seen of any survivors or bodies. We then carried on to the target.' Tom Henthorne was flying his last mission with 99 Squadron that day and it proved a fine finale:

'Large oil fires were started when we left, the whole area was blanketed in black smoke. On the way back to Dhubalia an airfield near the target area was strafed and hits were observed on a twin-engined aircraft.'

Leslie Parsons's crew were also in the air that

Above: *A 356 Squadron Liberator at dispersal near the shoreline on Cocos Island.*

Below: *Aerial view of the landing strip on Cocos' Island.*

day. They were briefed to bomb the railway bridge on the Bangkok-Singapore railway on the eastern side of the Malay Peninsula and as Parsons recalls, it was to prove their worst flying experience in South East Asia.

'We took off in *K* and straight away were in heavy rain and thick, low clouds. There was no chance of a loaded Liberator being able to climb over the top of Monsoon clouds so we flew at about 15,000 feet. Unfortunately, after about six hours' flying we flew straight into cumulo-nimbus clouds which were invisible to us. Cumulo-nimbus clouds with the anvil top rising to 25,000-30,000 feet have the most violent currents and have sufficient power to tear the wings from an aircraft.

'The first indication that we were in trouble came when the aircraft was thrown straight up at what seemed a colossal speed, while the pilot struggled to hold the nose down. The next sensation was an equally violent downward plunge followed by a feeling that we were going round and round within the cloud. Then we were suddenly thrown out of the cloud and we could see Malaya below. To our intense relief and astonishment the Liberator was still in one piece and we were able to descend and bomb the bridge.

'But the violence of cumulo-nimbus clouds had taken its toll and after two hours on our return journey the number two engine failed and had to be feathered. It was clear to us all that with the reduced performance and the appalling weather conditions we would never make the return trip to India. The aircraft would barely climb so we were forced whenever possible to fly just below the cloud base at between 500 and 1,000 feet.

'I told 'Mac' Baxter, my pilot, that we had no alternative but to head for Rangoon and pray that the airfield there was suitable for landing a Liberator. Many times it was necessary to make diversions to avoid cloud, storms, and islands suddenly appearing out of the rain. The entire crew was tense, flying for two to three hours at only 500 feet above the waves and knowing that the slightest trouble would send us into the sea. The tension only started to ease when we saw the sea beginning to turn brown about thirty miles from the Burmese coast. We realized this must be due to the sand and silt of the Irrawaddy Delta.

'We hit the Burmese coast just south of Rangoon about an hour before dark and made our way to Mingaladoon airfield a few miles north of the capital. We asked for permission to land and were told that the main runway, which could take a Liberator, was still pitted with bomb craters and only the short runway for fighters had been repaired. We had no option but to use the short runway. Thanks to 'Mac's' usual great skill we succeeded in landing within the limits (much to the surprise of those on the ground who took bets that we would go over drop at the end of the runway).

'On 20 June 1945 we were withdrawn from operations and assigned to special training, dropping containers on parachutes from low level (about 150 feet) on to a small area. The bombing range at Salbani in northern India was the main training area. Many rumours circulated concerning our impending operations; from dropping spies in Siam, to low-level attacks on highly secret targets or dropping paratroops on the Andaman Islands.'

All these rumours proved unfounded. With the demise of the Japanese forces in Burma focus of attention had switched to operations in Malaya and Sumatra. On 15 May 1945 No. 200 Squadron at Jessore, equipped with Liberator VIs, had been re-numbered No. 8 Squadron and, after moving to Ceylon a few days later, began making supply drops to guerrillas in Malaya and Sumatra together with No. 160 Squadron. One of the arrivals in Ceylon was Colin Berry, an air-gunner who had trained at Nassau in the Bahamas. In January 1945 he and

his fellow crew members, a former Coastal Command crew, flew to Minnerea, Ceylon to join 200 Squadron, which at that time was acting in a Special Duties capacity supplying Force 136 in Malaya and Sumatra. Berry recalls, 'At that time, to make room for more fuel, all the gunners, except the wireless-operator/air gunner, were dropped from the crew. During June 1945 an 8 Squadron Liberator established a world endurance record of 24 hours 10 minutes.'

On 16 July 1945 99 Squadron was briefed to fly to Kankesanturai airbase on the northern tip of Ceylon. Each Liberator was packed with ground crew and all essential equipment. Les Parsons's Liberator carried the kitchen staff and all their cooking utensils.

'We left Dhubalia and landed in Ceylon in the early afternoon and were told to report for a further briefing to our ultimate destination in the late afternoon. We still had no idea where we were going—it was such a well-kept secret. But when we entered the Briefing Room we saw the long strand on the map of the South Pacific indicating the track from Kankesanturai and travelling towards Australia, stopping about two thirds of the way in what seemed like 'open sea'.'

What appeared to be a tract of 'open sea' was in fact the Cocos or Keeling Islands, about 2,000 miles from Ceylon and 1,000 miles from Perth, Australia, or about ten degrees south of the Equator. The plan was for the Island group to be turned into a fortress for Operation 'Zipper', the intended invasion of Sumatra, Java, and Malaya. On 23 June 1945, Geoffrey Ely, Wing Navigation Officer and a member of 99 Squadron, had made a special flight in a Liberator to the islands. The flight took nine

and a half hours and the return ten .

Ely briefed the rest of the Squadron and at 19.00 hours on 16 July 1945 99 Squadron crews began taking off for the Cocos. They flew until dawn and all made the long trip safely. Les Parsons recalls, 'Failure to find the islands would have resulted in a watery grave but it was a thrill to finally see the white wall of water breaking on the coral reef.'

No. 99 Squadron shared the Cocos Islands base with the Liberators of No. 356 Squadron.

The direction of these Liberator operations was under the control of Army intelligence and a specially appointed Army officer carried out the briefings. He told the expectant crews that they were to drop arms and ammunition to guerrillas in the hills of Malaya in the Kuala Lumpur district. The guerrillas, consisting of Chinese Malays and escaped British and Australia POWs, were to assist in the eventual invasion of Malaya. Les Parsons remembers the supply dropping operations. 'I was involved in two operations; 'Tideway' and 'Funnel'. Both were long, unescorted trips across the Indian Ocean to Sumatra where we crossed over the mountain range on the west coast of the Island. We flew on across the low-lying part and over the Strait of Malacca to the Cameron highlands. Both the dropping zones had code-names and it was pretty difficult map reading. We were looking for a small clearing in the hills marked with a white letter 'H' aided by a small fire. We always flew in daylight to enable us to arrive at the D.Z. at around 16.00 hours so that the guerrillas could get back to their camps in the hills during darkness before the Japs could catch them. (It gets dark around 18.00 hours.)

'Having found the clearing we flew in at about 150 feet and dropped the containers. We always circled long enough to see the guerrillas rush from the trees, collect their containers and drag them away. We were low enough to wave to each other. We were then faced with the long return journey in darkness. The more difficult part being the climb over the huge cumulo-nimbus clouds which had been built up by equatorial heat on the mountains of western Sumatra.

Above: *A 99 Squadron (Madras Presidency) Liberator swirls up the dust during a take-off from Cocos. Engineers cleared the coconut trees and laid a metal lattice runway. All personnel slept in tents pitched alongside the coconut palms and only a few yards from the coral beaches.*

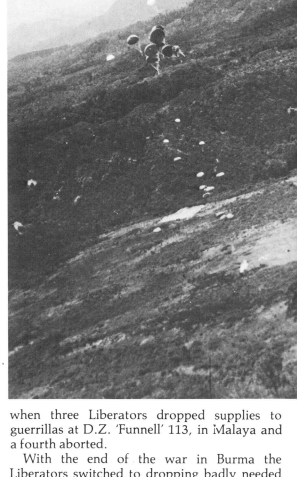

Left Top: Attacks on the infamous Burma-Siam railway were made throughout the war. Between January and April 1945 Eastern Air Command Liberators achieved an average of nine bridges down at any time between Bangkok and Burma. These attacks reduced rail traffic from 750 tons to 150 tons a day and in an effort to combat this the Japanese had to build reserve bridges; sometimes as many as four across strategic points. This photograph shows a 159 Squadron attack on two bridges.

Left Below: A 99 Squadron Liberator banks low over the Kuala Lumpur racecourse and releases its load of supplies on 5 September 1945.

Before plans could get under way for the invasion of Malaysia the first atomic bomb to be used in warfare was dropped on 6 August on Hiroshima. Three days later another was dropped on Nagasaki. The actions saved thousands of Allied lives who would otherwise have been lost in the invasion of Japan and its captured territories. On the morning of 10 August 1945 Japan sued for peace.

Four Liberator squadrons flew their final operations of the war during the first fortnight of August 1945. No. 356 flew its last combat mission on 6 August when three Liberators bombed and strafed Japanese aircraft at Benkulen. Next day 99, 159 and 355 Squadrons completed their tour of operations. Five Liberators from 159 Squadron attacked two bridges on the Siam-Burma railway. Four Liberators of 355 Squadron were also involved in the bombing of the railway, in the Bangkok area, after their primary target of shipping off the east coast of the Kra Isthmus had been aborted. The 'railway of death' had cost the lives of 24,000 Allied POWs involved in its enforced construction. Meanwhile four Liberators from 99 Squadron blasted two Japanese airfields south-east of Benkoelen.

Five days later, on 12 August, 99 Squadron flew its final operational mission of the war

when three Liberators dropped supplies to guerrillas at D.Z. 'Funnell' 113, in Malaya and a fourth aborted.

With the end of the war in Burma the Liberators switched to dropping badly needed food and medical supplies to thousands of beleaguered Allied prisoners of war scattered throughout the Far East. Their Japanese and Korean captors had resorted to the lowest forms of bestiality and depravity during their long imprisonment. Many had been in captivity for almost four years and almost all were walking skeletons. The Japanese, in many cases, had not even needed to erect barbed wire to keep the prisoners captive. The jungle was a natural barrier and lack of food and disease sapped the POWs' strength and will, making escape virtually impossible.

On 28 August both 99 and 356 Squadrons took part in 'Operation Birdcage' when crews officially began dropping leaflets to POW camps in and around Singapore. Unofficially, crews dropped all the cigarettes and clothing they could obtain on the Cocos.

The sight of Liberators flying low over their camps dropping their very welcome supplies brought overwhelming relief. But the drops were not without cost. During a drop at Sungei Ron POW camp at Palembang in Sumatra by a

99 Squadron Liberator, an entire crew met their deaths when their aircraft crashed. The POWs conducted a funeral with all the resources at their disposal and the crew were buried with full military honours. The effect on the POWs was such that no one could look at a low-flying aircraft for days afterwards. Among those in the camp who saw the crash were five survivors from a 215 Squadron (RAF) Liberator crew shot down on 14 August 1945 in the Sunda Strait. By September 1945 the emaciated POWs were being flown out almost daily to Singapore. That month the main body of the British relief force arrived by sea and the remaining POWs were taken aboard.

In addition to transport duties the Liberators of 159 and 355 Squadrons participated in 'Operation Hunger', the ferrying or dropping of rice to the starving population of South Burma. Rice cultivation in the hill districts of Burma had suffered heavily during the Japanese occupation and what little was grown was sufficient only for the natives' immediate needs. In the Delta valleys the crops were plentiful but with the transport system in ruins there was little hope of transferring the rice other than by air. From September 1945 until early 1946 159 dropped one and a half million pounds of rice in 486 sorties.

On 15 November 1945 Nos. 8, 99, and 356 Squadrons disbanded. C. Berry recalls: 'Most of 8 Squadron's Liberators were flown back to various central units in India, among them 308 M.U. at Cawnpore in the Central Plains, and just broken up. It seemed to us at the time to be a waste of perfectly good aircraft, some with less than fifty hours' flying time on the clock.'

In early 1946 159 and 355 Squadrons were also disbanded. After their rice dropping missions the two squadrons shared an aerial survey assignment on behalf of the Government of Bengal and then on 30 April 1946 159 Squadron ceased to exist. One month later, on 31 May 1946, 355 Squadron also disbanded. Meanwhile, 160 Squadron continued food and mail deliveries to the Cocos Islands and other transport duties, until in June 1946 it returned to England and began re-equipping with Lancasters.

During combat operations from Burma, ground crews had performed miracles in often appalling conditions and with limited equipment and spare parts to keep the Liberators operational. These magnificent highly-adaptable bombers had served the RAF faithfully in the Far East; an airborne theatre of operations often forgotten by Press, public, and historian alike.

Centre: *Liberators of 356 Squadron bringing relief in the form of aerial supplies to a POW camp somewhere in Burma on 6 September 1945. The day after drops, two-man liaison teams were always parachuted in to assist with recovery.*

Right Top: *An aerial view of discarded Liberators at Chakeri, Cawnpore, India, after the end of the war.*

Right Below: *Liberators await the scrap-yard or transfer to the Indian Air Force.*

Over the Hills and Far Away

Left Top: *In the spring of 1941 BOAC began operating seven Liberators carrying supplies and VIPs eastbound over the Atlantic and returning with much needed airmen. By September 1941 the entire Return Ferry service passed to BOAC under whose organization provided a transport service for RAF pilots to the requirements of RAF Ferry Command. By February 1946 BOAC had flown its 2,000th flight.*

Left Centre: *Liberator Mark III (ex FL417) at Prestwick in January 1944. This particular aircraft was one of five used by BOAC on the Lisbon, West Africa and Stockholm services from November 1942 until they were all returned to the RAF in January 1945.*

Left Bottom: *A BOAC Return Ferry Service Liberator on the snow covered runway during winter operations from Dorval, Canada. In the late 1940s BOAC used Liberators on non-stop flights from Montreal to London refuelled en-route by Lancaster tankers.*

Top: *Liberator C-109 'Flying Tankers' at one of the Indian bases of the India-China division of Air Transport Command. These aircraft, together with C-87s and other converted Liberators delivered more than 15 per cent of the 5,327 tons of material flown over the 'Hump' on the record breaking day 1 August 1944.*

Left: *A rare silver B-24D of the 308th BG 14th AF at Kunming, China, takes off over the heads of Chinese wagons. C-47s and C-46 Commandos proliferate on the airfield perimeter. The 308th was the only Liberator bomber outfit to operate from China.*

Wings of Gold
Paul Stevens

When the United States were drawn into the war in December 1941 the Convair PBY Catalina flying boat was already an old sea dog. Later it was supplemented by the PB2Y 'Coronado' also from the Convair stable, and the Martin PBM 'Mariner'. Convair's successful PB2Y design was easily adapted to a land-based bomber design, the B-24, but its sea-going pedigree and 3,000 mile range was just what the US Navy was looking for to extend the range beyond that of the amphibious aircraft then in service. The PB4Y-1 was commissioned for US Navy service. Fortress crews nicknamed the B-24 the 'Banana Boat' because of its flying-boat ancestry. They said the B-24 'had been designed as a flying boat but they couldn't plug the leaks and turned it into a bomber instead!' But the PB4Y-1 was to prove an ideal aircraft in the Pacific for sea search and patrol and packed a punch that the Japanese came to respect.

The PB4Y-1 looked like a Liberator; it had almost all the features of the B-24 including the twin-tail empennage and was just as lethal. However, there the similarity ended. Navy pilots, trained at Norfolk, Hutchinson, and San Diego, were not pilots as such but PPCs: Patrol Plane Commanders. Of course Navy and Army ranks differed but the bell-bottomed bomber crews earned the distinction of being able to tackle almost any job on the PB4Y-1. Pilots were equally at home with navigational duties and vice-versa while gunners usually boasted secondary trades like maintenance and even metal working. Every member of the crew was a rated air gunner, trained to take over any of the gun positions.

The first Navy patrol squadron to be equipped with the Liberator was VP-101, which flew their B-24D models to Barbers Point Naval Air Station on Oahu, T.H. At about this time

VP-102 and a Marine photo squadron also flew out to the forward area. In the spring of 1943 they were supplemented by Navy Photo Squadron VD-1 (V being the code for heavier than air and so equally incongruously, D for Photographic).

On 10 April 1943 VP 104 was commissioned at Naval Air Station, Kaneohe Bay, T.H. with Lieutenant-Commander Harry E. Sears as Commanding Officer. Formation of the squadron resulted from splitting VP 21 in half, thereby immediately creating a unit experienced in flying PBY-5 aircraft. By mid July all the air crews were proficient in all operational procedures and a month later were sent to Carney Field, Guadalcanal to form the first Navy Long Range Search Group with VP 102. In July 1943 Lieutenant-Commander Bruce Van Voorhis was in charge of VP 102 during the Battle of the Solomon Islands. On 6 July he and his crew took off on the 700 mile flight, alone and in total darkness, for the Japanese-held Greenwich Island to help prevent a surprise enemy attack on American forces. Despite treacherous and varying winds, limited visibility and difficult terrain, the crew got through to their target, a seaplane tender off Kapingamarangi (a small atoll north-west of the Solomons). Van Voorhis was forced lower and lower by overwhelming aerial opposition. Despite this the gallant crew executed six low-level attacks, destroying the Japanese radio

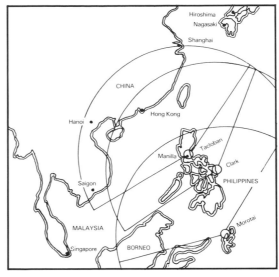

station, anti-aircraft guns and other installations with bombs and machine gun fire. Voorhis's gunners destroyed one Japanese fighter in the air and another three on the ground. Caught in his own bomb blast, Van Voorhis and his crew crashed into the lagoon off the beach and perished. For his sacrifice and lone fight against insuperable odds Lieutenant-Commander Van Voorhis was posthumously awarded America's highest decoration, the Medal of Honor.

Meanwhile, 104 and 102, now under the command of Lieutenant-Commander Gordon

Left: *PB4Y-1s on patrol over the Pacific. Together with PB4Y-2s they hunted surface vessels and submersibles. Although not designed for Naval patrolling, they revitalized the ailing patrol bomber squadrons, making usually unescorted strikes way out into the wastes of the Pacific.*

Centre and Right: *On 14 December 1944 Lieutenant Paul Stevens's crew scored direct hits with 100 lb incendiaries on each of two heavily camouflaged 200 ton Sugar Dogs laden with oil drums sinking both of them.*

Fowler, continued operations against the enemy in the Pacific. In addition to their primary role of daily search and tracing of enemy task force units a large number of formation strikes were made against land targets and one strike against a Japanese destroyer fleet. Individual strikes were made when the opportunity arose. Burton Albrecht and his crew made a lone strike on a convoy of nine armed cargo ships, sinking three and fending off fourteen fighters. His claimed three 'kills'. He also avenged Voorhis's death with an attack on Kapingamarangi, sinking six Zero floatplanes from among the dozen or so high and dry on the beach.

On 6 February 1944 VPB 104 moved to Munda Field, New Georgia where it continued operations until the end of March 1944 when it was relieved by VPB 115. VPB 104 had flown well over a thousand sorties, destroying or damaging thirty aircraft and fifty-one enemy surface vessels for the loss of only seven Liberators. VPB 104 returned Stateside for leave and reformation and was subsequently awarded the Presidential Unit Citation.

On 15 May 1944 VPB 104 was re-formed at Naval Air Station, Kearney Mesa, California. Training was carried out until late June 1944 with Lieutenant Henry S. Noon as Acting Commanding Officer. During that time many new personnel arrived, bringing with them expertise gained flying with other units in the long and arduous Pacific campaign. One such officer was Lieutenant Paul Stevens. In 1941 he had reported to his first duty station at Pearl Harbor and was actually on his way to battle stations at Wake Island in a PBY Catalina when the war broke out for the United States. Stevens went on to fly operations in the Australia-New Guinea area against the Japanese. Using Catalinas he made night missions against the 'Tokio Express', and airfields in the Rabaul area. He returned to the States in November 1943, later transferring to the redesignated VPB 104 which in the summer of 1944 came under the command of Lieutenant-Commander Whitney Wright. On 30 October 1944, after months of intensive training and familiarization flights, VPB 104 began its move to the Pacific war zone, at Morotai in the Netherlands East Indies. Paul Stevens, now Squadron Executive, and his crew, spent the stop-over wisely, sanding down the dark blue upper surfaces and light blue undersurfaces of their Liberator for two days, 'borrowing' two gallons of floor wax from the VOQ and spending two more days waxing down the entire aircraft. When they had finished Stevens reckoned that it would add between five and ten knots to their speed.

On 3 November the 'Buccaneers of Screaming 104' arrived at Morotai after bucking bad weather fronts *en route*, to relieve VPB 115, which had originally relieved the Buccaneers. VPB 104 and VPB 101, also equipped with Liberators, and VPB 146, equipped with PV-1s, now formed the Navy Search Group attached to the US Seventh Fleet. Morotai was anything but peaceful and crews were 'welcomed' on the first night by a large air raid. By the end of the month this had been followed by a further forty-five attacks. Day and night artillery- and mortar-fire could be heard near the Japanese lines close by. Skirmishes and infiltrations made for little sound sleep and crews kept their sidearms close by at all times. There were other diversions, too, like the appearance of large lithesome pythons around the tents and 'Long Tom' trees which were brought down on living quarters by strong winds.

But 'Whit' Wright soon had his men organized and preparations were made to get the eighteen flight crews and fifteen Liberators ready for combat. On 6 November Whitney Wright made the first flight from Morotai and

successfully intercepted a 150 ton lugger. He achieved three direct hits with 250 lb bombs and the ninety-foot-long craft sank immediately. Another lugger, loaded with oil drums, was also sighted and repeated fire from Wright's gunners soon had it alight from end to end. It burned fiercely until it sank. But on 11 November 1944 Lieutenant Maurice Hill was attacked by two Tonys while on regular patrol and his bomber hit the water and broke up. Only four of the eleven-man crew survived and were rescued by friendly natives.

Paul Stevens recalls, 'Our missions were described as 'armed reconnaissance' which meant that we flew single plane missions, initially 800 nautical miles out and 100 mile cross leg and back. Later they were extended to 1000 miles out. Normally we carried from 1000 to 2000 pounds of bombs in various loads and we could do anything we had the guts to do.

The two forward bomb bays had two 300 gallon tanks in them and we carried bombs only in the two aft bomb bays. We also carried an awful lot of spare 0.50 calibre machine guns and on occasions, extra 100lb bombs and just lay them in the fuselage. These were particularly effective against the small Japanese shipping which we called, 'Sugar Puppies', 'Sugar Dogs' and 'Sugar Charlies', which were around 1500 tons and carried an awful lot of commerce for the Japanese. But they were very easy meat for us.

'Our range at that time was in excess of 2100 nautical miles on combat missions which included some time at combat power, running at 45 inches and 2500 rpm. Our favourite targets were the small wooden luggers and 'Sugar Dogs'. Occasionally we would come up against a convoy and if we felt we had surprise we would not go ahead and make an attack,

A US Navy PB4Y-1 over the Philippines.

but would go in at 'mast head' height. Our bombs were fused with a five-second delay action and if we had surprise we would make a run against quite large ships.

'Of course there were times when we were surprised. One such occasion occurred on 12 November 1944, the first time I made a convoy attack. There were two 'Fox Tare Bakers' (freight transports) escorted by three destroyers and a gunboat near Baguit Bay, Palawan Island. I came around a point of land and there was this convoy. It was a calm day and the water was very still. I immediately asked for 45 inches, auto rich and started a run in. We flew so low on the water we actually left a wake from our down wash. I started on the centre ship, which was probably about 10,000 tons. At first I thought I had him by complete surprise but as I closed in I saw smoke drifting up. I though, "Oh Crap! I've picked the wrong ship, he's already been hit." But I suddenly realised he hadn't been hit; it was gun fire aimed at me! We were in so close I was actually looking upwards at him! I pulled up over him and released two 500 lb bombs and five 100 lb bombs, all of which I believe, hit him. We were hit, too, how badly I didn't know, but I could hear shrapnel going through the 'plane. I threw the 'plane over in a violent skid and got right back down on the water and misled the gunners on the escort ships which now confronted us. Going out from the convoy I crossed an escort ship at extremely low level. My gunners opened up at point-blank range, hitting the steam line to his whistle among other things because a big plume of steam rose into the air. The anti-aircraft fire hit the bow turret, wounding the bow gunner, Derral Pedigo, and wounding the bombardier, Lee Webber. All four engines remained running and there appeared to be no fuel leaks. I climbed and got behind some high hills and headed on home after taking some photographs.

'About two hours after I landed back at Morotai another plane from the squadron came upon the ship I had hit and a destroyer which had remained behind while the rest of the convoy had pulled out. Two large explosions ripped the ship apart and I was credited with its sinking.'

After less than two months' operations from Morotai the Buccaneers prepared to follow the advance north to Leyte, where 'Screaming 104' came under the new command of Fleet Air Wing Ten. On 9 December fourteen crews flew to Tacloban on Leyte, which was to be their new home, and were joined by the remaining four crews later that month. Although everyone was not sorry to leave Morotai, Tacloban was not without its problems as Paul Stevens recalls:

'Tacloban was the only Allied air strip in operation in the area and consisted of a single strip built of lashed steel matting and laid on loose sand. The traffic was extremely heavy

and every available inch of parking space was in use. In addition to the regular parking space, airplanes were parked wing tip to wing tip on each side of the runway. This allowed only about thirty feet of wing tip clearance for take off and landing.

'The PB4Y-1 was an excellent airplane but we were flying it in a heavily overloaded condition. The airplane had originally been designed for a gross operating weight of 56,000 lbs. It had been cleared for an overload weight of 63,000 lb and further cleared for an emergency war overload to 65,000 lb. We were operating the airplane at 68,000 lb gross weight. Therefore, every take-off, normally undertaken at pre-dawn, was quite an experience. The loose lashed matting on the sand base created an up-hill run on every take off.'

The area of search from Leyte included two sectors extending to Cap San Jacques and Camranh Bay, French Indo-China, another sector to Balabao Strait and down the west coast of Borneo. Other sectors covered the area from Hainan Strait up the coast of China to Foochow and eastward to include Okinawa and Daito Jima. During the first few days at their new base a number of VPB 104 crews made repeated attacks on Japanese shipping and aircraft.

On 2 December Lieutenant Ray Ettinger sighted a convoy of six ships north of Balikpapan, Borneo. He went in about four miles off the convoy and was fired upon, first by one of the ships and then by three Oscars. They open fire at 600 yards, making a co-ordinated attack from 3, 5, and 9 o'clock. They closed to 200 yards but the Liberator's return fire forced them to climb 1,500 feet above the bomber. The Oscars dropped four phosphorous bombs dead ahead of Ettinger but they exploded 200 feet distant at about 8 o'clock. For thirty minutes the Oscars made high side and tail runs before the PB4Y-1 was able to lose them in cloud.

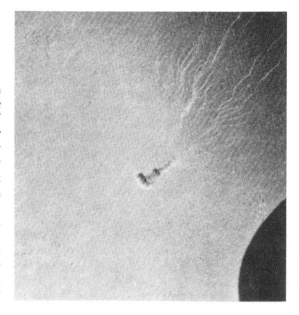

A phosphorous bomb dropped on Lieutenant Stevens's plane on 8 December 1944.

Dropping phosphorus bombs on American aircraft was a favourite Japanese ploy and it was Paul Stevens's turn to be on the receiving end six days later. He was returning from a patrol down the Makassar Straits when a seaplane base was spotted at Toli Toli Bay, Celebes. Four Petes were on the water and two were airborne. Stevens made a low strafing run, destroying one Pete on the water and probably destroying another, they were parked wing tip to wing tip. During the strafing run the two airborne Petes dived down for an attack and dropped two aerial bombs which burst fairly close to the PB4Y-1. One of them appeared to be a phosphorous bomb and it spread underneath the bomber. The Petes continued their attack with high side passes on either quarter and a running fight lasting about twenty minutes ensued. One of the Petes broke off after only a few minutes, streaming smoke and on the last run made by the other Pete the rear gunner was missing, his gun sticking straight up before the plane disappeared into cloud.

Two days later, on 10 December, Lieutenant Henry S. Noon's PB4Y-1 was attacked by eight Zekes (Zeros) and two Tonys which dropped a total of eight phosphorous bombs, some of which burst very close to Noon's aircraft. He managed to reach safety after a running fight involving head-on attacks and passes from every position on the clock lasting for about an hour. One Zeke was definitely destroyed, bursting into flames as it hit the water and two more limped away from the scene trailing smoke after being hit in the engines and wing roots.

The Japanese airmen, already at a disadvantage flying without armour plate, soon learned to respect the PB4Y-1s and their devastating fire power. The day after Noon's attack Paul Stevens showed the Japs just what a Liberator's gunners could do when he found a flotilla of ten seaplanes napping at Puerto Princessa. He made four strafing runs and the gunners destroyed two Jakes and two Petes and damaged another four.

When ships could not be found the PB4Y-1 crews sought targets inland. On 12 December Lieutenant Joseph D. Shea's crew bombed and

A PB4Y-1 of the US Navy, photographed in 1942.

Left Top: *Lieutenant
Stevens and Lieutenant
Woodford W. Sutherland
each attacked a 5,300 ton
FTB escorted by a destroyer
and a gunboat. Sutherland
made the first attack using
the clouds and a 35-knot
wind to good advantage.
On the first run a 500 lb
bomb was released
manually, but fell short and
exploded about 40 feet off
the stern. Sutherland made
a second run, again using the
northerly tail-wind and
dropped two 500 pounders.
One hit the base of the
bridge, knocking off the
stack and exploding below
decks. The other bomb
went through the fantail
and exploded 10 feet off the
stern. All bombs gone
Sutherland called up
Lieutenant Stevens from
another sector and the two
Libs rendezvoused at 13.00
to continue the attack.
Stevens dropped ten 100 lb
bombs scoring seven direct
hits. Both planes strafed the
ship with about 4,700
rounds of 0.50 calibre API
and left the ship burning
and listing, dead in the
water. The crew abandoned
ship. On 24 January 1945
Sutherland's Liberator
crashed into Tacloban Bay
on take-off killing five of
the crew and seriously
injuring Sutherland and
two others.*

Left Bottom: *Paul Stevens's
crew shoot down a Val on
31 December 1944.*

Right Top: *When shipping
targets were fogged off or
could not be found crews
struck inland. On 27
November 1944 Lieutenant
Stevens, after searching the
harbours in Borneo, and
carrying no bombs due to
the length of the search,
found and strafed a seven-
car train running along the
coast causing a large
volume of steam to be
emitted in various
directions from the
locomotive and bringing
the train to a stop.
However, not all PB4Y-1
crews were lucky over land.
One crew, shot down over
Japanese-held territoty,
crouched in gulleys beside
the road near their crashed
Liberator. An enemy
column approached and
one half of the crew in a
gully on one side of the
road surrendered. They
were beheaded on the spot.
The remaining members
melted into the jungle.*

strafed numerous targets in and around Brunei
Town, Borneo. First he attacked an airstrip
under construction and then a motor convoy
loaded with troops. Proceeding on over the
harbour Shea made three bombing and strafing
runs on shipping, setting a 1,500 ton 'Sugar
Charlie' on fire and damaging other ships and
luggers. Return fire put many holes in the
PB4Y-1, holing a fuel line from the main wing
cell and filling the aircraft with fumes. Five
crew members were overcome by the fumes and
the bomb-bay door was opened to secure some
fresh air. William E. Abbott passed out while
transferring fuel by holding the connection
together by hand. He became unconscious and
fell through the bomb-bay door from an
altitude of 1,500 feet over Borneo. All the other
crew members later recovered after treatment
at base.

On 26 December 1944 Paul Stevens was
allocated the patrol sector west of Leyte
stretching to Camranh Bay in French Indo-
China. It was to prove a momentous mission as
Stevens recalls:

'I lined the airplane up on the runway, in
utter darkness except for a few flare pots to
light the edge of the runway, and applied full
power. The airplane accelerated very slowly as
we ran down the airstrip which was only about
two feet above the water. Slowly our speed
increased and as we approached the end of the
strip, the airplane literally fell off and it was
hoped we had sufficient air speed to start
flying.

'For about one minute we skimmed close to
the water, gradually building up air speed. If an
engine failed or even coughed we would have
been in the water. Once we had got the gear
retracted and had gained a little altitude, we
could finally breathe just a little bit easier. We
left maximum power on and began climbing
across the mountains of the central Philippine
Islands, heading westward across Cebu, Panay,
Mindoro and across the South China Sea to
Camranh Bay in French Indo-China.

'Once achieving 3,000 feet altitude, we set a
westward course and continued climbing to
about 8,000 feet. During the climb in our
heavily overloaded airplane, the cylinder head
temperatures ran extremely high. It was a
continual battle to keep up the climb and at the
same time maintain an adequate air speed to
keep the engines from completely overheating.
The engines on the PB4Y-1 were very closely
cowled to permit the greatest aerodynamic
efficiency and at the same time permit adequate
cooling. However, in this overloaded condition
when climbing with high power, the engines
would invariably overheat. Opening cowl flaps
to control the cylinder head temperatures could
spoil lift across the wing and consequently
reduce the rate of climb. So in the end, the
climb out of Leyte to get above the mountains
was a continual play of air speed, power, and
opening cow flaps to get the airplane to the
altitude desired. During this climb, I required
the crewmen to maintain their positions in the
airplane and allowed no opening of gun ports
or swinging of gun turrets that would spoil lift
or upset the balance of flight.

'Once reaching cruising altitude of 8,000 feet
the after fuselage gun station hatches could be
opened and the guns swung out. In addition,
our radar gear on this particular airplane
consisted of a radome that could be retracted
into the bottom of the fuselage. After reaching
cruising altitude the radome was extended and
our search begun. I recall on this flight as I
approached the Island of Mindoro dawn was
just beginning to break. I was well established
on my search sector, all gun stations manned,
my radar gear in operation, and ready for any
eventuality. During the climb and cruise

toward the Island of Mindoro, we were in and out of clouds, and I had been briefed to expect heavy weather throughout the entire patrol. The amphibious landings at Mindoro had just recently been accomplished. As was always the case in newly acquired real estate, this was expected to be a hot area. For a Navy patrol plane to operate singly and proceed through a hot area, we could expect almost anything. Japanese aircraft would be contesting the landings and as usual, our own ships and land-based AA batteries were not reluctant to open fire on anything with wings on. Our own fighters had on occasion shot up our aircraft due to poor recognition or just over-eagerness on the part of the pilots. As was my practice, as we approached this hit area, I told my crew to fire upon any approaching hostile aircraft.

'Just prior to approaching this area, all guns had been test fired and were in good working order. In addition, I had shifted by VHF radio to the frequency that I knew the fighters were being controlled on in this area. I called the fighter interceptor stations and told them I was proceeding through their area. It was dawn and fighters were just being launched as a Japanese air raid was in progress on the Island. I was therefore unable to establish communications. As I followed the action over Mindoro by listening to the vectoring of friendly fighters, it appeared to me that we might meet Japanese aircraft returning from their strikes while passing over the northern part of the Island. Although the crew was alerted and we had hopes of perhaps engaging a straggler, we made no contacts.

Right Bottom: *Lieutenant Paul Stevens's crew: Back Row, Left to Right; Allen Anania, Radio-op/Gunner; David Gleason, Mechanic/Gunner; Lee Webber, Plane Captain; Lee Little, Ordnance/Gunner; Adrian Fox, Radioman/Gunner; Arvid Rasmussen, Mechanic/Gunner; Front Row, Left to Right: Marx Stephan, Ordnanceman; Lieutenant John McKinley, Co-pilot; Lieutenant Paul Stevens, Plane Commander; Lieutenant Ed Streit, First Pilot; Derral Pedigo, Mechanic/Gunner.*

119

A series of three photos showing Paul Stevens's crew shooting up Japanese floatplanes in Camranh Bay on 26 December 1944.

'We were under orders to make no attacks and no bombs were carried. This was necessary, as I understood it, because of the landings on Mindoro. There was the absolute requirement that we cover our sectors as thoroughly as possible. On some previous occasions our patrol planes when proceeding outbound on their search sectors, had engaged the enemy and on occasion were damaged to the degree that they were forced to return to base and consequently unable to cover their sectors. This as a general rule made the Wing Commander and the Commander, Air Forces Seventh Fleet, most unhappy. However, our mission was truly Armed Reconnaissance, and as such we usually went out heavily loaded with bombs and additional 50 calibre ammunition. Our operating principle was to attack any target of opportunity that we felt we could adequately handle. My own personal feeling at this time was that the ordinary hazard of flying this heavily loaded airplane under the conditions we were operating made it mandatory that I initiate attacks at every opportunity. To date, myself and my crew had engaged in many, many actions and we had numerous enemy aircraft and ships to our credit. We had been damaged and had men wounded during these actions, but in every case we were able to complete our missions. The effort and men and material required to keep us in the forward area further demanded that we attack at every opportunity. Just prior to this patrol, while operating temporarily under the instructions of no attacks, against these instructions I had my airplane fully loaded with bombs and had made several successful shipping attacks. I was mildly rebuked by the Air Wing Intelligence Officers, but inasmuch as we had gained several kills, it appeared to me to be more in jest than in seriousness.

'Once we cleared the Mindoro area, we ran into extremely heavy weather. The turbulence was violent and we were in and out of extremely heavy rain. It should be noted that our radar was ineffective in areas of heavy rain. With this type of radar, heavy rain showers would give returns on the scope and blank out large areas. As we continued across the South China Sea, these same weather conditions existed. I realized that my search in this area was only partially effective. However, there was no other choice but to continue and hope for a reduction in the intensity of the rain squalls or even clearing weather. As we approached the French Indo-China coast, I descended to a lower altitude. It was my policy that where possible I would always be on the water in areas where I could expect fighter opposition. I had the utmost confidence in my airplane and crew that we could handle ourselves against any number of Japanese fighters provided we were not caught at a high altitude. At the French Indo-China coast, the

weather had improved somewhat and consisted of a heavy overcast with some showers. Outside of showers the visibility was good.

As we approached Camranh Bay, it was my decision to proceed into the Bay far enough to insure a complete investigation. It was from Camranh Bay that a major portion of the Japanese fleet sortied for the Second Battle of the Philippine Sea. As we approached the fleet anchorage area, I advanced throttles to maximum power and started a run in at very low altitude. At the entrance to the Bay a small vessel, apparently an anti-submarine vessel was steaming out. I passed him by and went on into the anchorage. As we approached the operating base, nine Jakes were sighted on the water. The Jake was a twin float, single engine airplane and carried a crew of three. It was normally used for anti-submarine patrols. They were 'easy meat' for a B-24 and we were generally

delighted to find them. I continued the high speed run just off the water and told my crew to open fire at will. One airplane was slowly taxiing out and as we approached and began firing on him all three men jumped into the sea and left the airplane taxiing off under its own power. Our strafing pass was close enough that I could see the three men had on heavy winter flying-suits. My thought at the time was "They are going to be cold in that water." We continued our strafing pass on the other anchored Jakes. My top and bow turret gunners seemed to be hitting very well. However, I noticed that the starboard waist gunner was firing into the buildings on the beach rather than at the aircraft.

'As a general rule, I always believed during an attack of this nature, that it was best to make one pass and keep right on going. It was amazing what a single airplane could get away with without sustaining damaged if it made a high-speed run in at extremely low altitude, made its firing or bombing pass, and continued right on. It was on the second and third and maybe even fourth pass that the boys generally got shot up. In this case, however, there was no return fire and once we passed the seaplane anchorage area, I put the airplane into an extreme bank and pulled hard to turn around as quickly as possible. I came back for my second firing pass and again all guns were firing in good order and my turrets seemed to be hitting quite frequently. One plane was sinking and another had a list. However, none of the seaplanes were burning. This upset me considerably as we could claim no kills unless the planes burned. Upon completing this firing pass, I found myself over the beach and was about to reverse course for a third firing pass. However, on a ridge just beyond the buildings and slightly above, I glanced down and saw about eight gun stations and Japanese madly scrambling about to man these guns. With this unhappy sight, I continued outbound and no more firing runs were made in this area.

'Looking back, we could see that one plane had sunk and two others were listing, and the airplane that had been abandoned was continuing merrily on its way with no crew aboard. Consequently, I claimed one airplane destroyed and two damaged. I really felt, however, that we had damaged more aircraft than this, and the probability was good that the two aircraft that were listing would probably sink. Evidently these aircraft were not serviced with fuel. Otherwise we could possibly have burned four of them.

'I then proceeded North bound along the French Indo-China coast. My radar was sweeping offshore and I was searching the Bay's inlets for additional Japanese shipping. The weather continued to be very marginal. However, about sixty miles north of Camranh Bay, I sighted three small tankers and one large

anchored in a bay. Further north, at Natrang airstrip we sighted a group of Japanese apparently having a personnel inspection. Quite a number of them were lined up in their whites in front of their hangars. However, Natrang airstrip was known to have strong AA defence, and we passed by quickly and continued with our search. As I have stated previously, at low altitudes I considered myself capable of beating off a fighter attack, but at the same time we frequently came upon targets of opportunity and passed them by before we were able to bring our guns to bear.

'Just north of the this airstrip we turned back towards Leyte and began out flight back home. I again climbed to about 8,000 feet and set up for maximum range cruise. Once again we entered the area of extremely heavy weather and I realized that this portion of the search would be somewhat sketchy. Approximately 170 miles west of Mindoro at 4:10 in the afternoon, we broke into the clear and I saw a sight that will live with me forever. This was the force that I originally identified as one battleship, one heavy cruiser, one light cruiser, and five destroyers. These ships were steaming at an extremely high speed, and had they not been enemy, they would have indeed been a beautiful sight. The heavy ship which I originally called a battleship was in actuality the heavy cruiser *Ashigara*, and the other heavy vessel was the light cruiser *Oyodo*. However, a common failing among all pilots, we invariably over-estimated the class of ship. It should be pointed out, however, that the Japanese heavy cruisers were considerably larger than our heavy cruisers, and consequently it was an easy mistake to call a Japanese heavy cruiser a battleship.

'My first reaction upon sighting the ships was one of extreme urgency, as I realized that this force was steaming towards our landing force on the beaches of Mindoro. I immediately told my crew to be alert for enemy fighters and had my radioman send out a flash message in plain language conveying that an enemy force of major importance had been sighted. Position of this force was only a short distance from the Japanese airfield complexes at Manila. I fully expected to be immediately attacked by a strong force of enemy fighters. This would have been most unfortunate, as we were cruising at about 8,000 feet and it would have been a long hard fight to get down to the water. And as I had said previously, being caught high by fighters was almost always fatal for a single patrol plane.

'I identified the ships as to class and had the navigator plot their position and we quickly made up a contact report. Of course this was all happening at the same time and I suppose these Japanese were as surprised to see me as I was to see them. Therefore within a very short time, about a minute after first sighting, the Japanese heavy cruiser opened fire with its main batteries. This was customary of heavy units of the Japanese fleet. With their main batteries they could reach out to extreme range. And if nothing else, it increased the aviator's respect for these forces.

'As a Naval aviator and particularly a patrol plane pilot, I realized that this was what I had been training for during my entire time in the Navy. It was now my problem to get my message off immediately to alert our forces. Unknown to me at this time was the fact that our support forces at Mindoro had withdrawn to replenish. Our amphibious forces were still there in large numbers building up supplies on the beach-head. They were extremely vulnerable to a force of this nature. Japanese cruisers are beautiful vessels, big, fast, and sleek, and I was quite shaken to find such a strong enemy force so close to our new beachhead.

'As I turned towards Mindoro, I increased power and had my radioman transmit the contact report several times in plain language to ensure that the message was received and understood. As I approached the Island I was able to contact the ground forces there on voice radio. They were naturally quite concerned, and we confirmed the position of the force. At this time another report evidently came in from some Army Air Corps B-25s of an amphibious force proceeding towards the landing area. I assured the forces at Mindoro, however, that there were no amphibious forces within this task force. I was asked to land at Mindoro to confirm my report and verify its composition.

'As I approached Mindoro, I could see that the amphibious forces were making preparations to get under way. The amphibious forces consisted of LSTs, LCIs, LCMs, and Liberty and Victory ships. I realized that these ships would have no chance whatsoever against this Japanese task force. I approached the temporary air strip where some Air Corps fighters had been operating. This air strip was merely a short strip bulldozed out with no surface on the dirt. There were very few planes on the strip. I came in for a landing and as I rolled out on the landing, my heavy airplane sank into the dirt to such a degree that a high power was required to keep it moving. I shut the airplane down and told the crew to immediately refuel it. Personnel at the airstrip did not want to refuel the airplane or even stay around the airstrip as a red alert was in effect at the time and the Japanese were attacking the airfield intermittently. I proceeded to the operation tent on the airstrip and telephoned the headquarters of the Army Corps that was ashore. I spoke with a Colonel who appeared to be in command at the time. He discussed the location and several questions about the composition of the Japanese force. He was particularly interested in whether or not amphibious forces were with the task force or in the area. At the conclusion of our talk, he

requested that I proceed to attack the force. I told him my mission was search, and I thought it would be best and that my command would desire that I track this force throughout the night. He replied that it was a matter of life or death for the personnel on the beach and requested that I go out and pick off a destroyer. To myself, I got quite a laugh out of the term "Picking off a destroyer", as with a force of this nature it would be extremely close going to even fly within gun range. This is particularly so for a single airplane. However, I appreciated the situation and decided to go ahead and launch the attack. I requested that the Colonel arrange to send me four 500 lb bombs immediately as I knew that this strip was hot so to speak, and I wanted to get off. I returned to the airplane and only a couple of my crew members were near the airplane. They said they had refuelled, but no bombs had arrived yet. They further advised me that some Army troops were in the immediate area and would give me something to eat if I desired. I was extremely tired and I had not eaten all day.

'I returned to the aircraft and about the same time the bomb-handling truck arrived with my four 500 lb bombs. It was getting dark at this point and the Japanese air attacks were increasing in intensity. About this time a P-38 crash-landed on the strip and stopped just in front of my airplane. This in effect reduced the runway length by about 1,000 feet. I became more and more concerned as to whether we would be able to get off in the short distance remaining. A couple of Army B-25s were near by and I could see that the pilots were preparing to man their aircraft. As I felt reasonably sure that they would be attacking this task force, I went over to discuss the possibility with them of a joint attack. At the time I arrived their flight leader, a Captain, had just informed the pilots that they were going to launch an attack against this force. This same flight of about twelve B-25s had started out earlier for a strike against an airfield in the Manila area. They had sighted this Japanese task force sometime after I had and had began an attack but because of the strong opposition had broken it off. When they were told by their flight leader that they must return for another attack against this force, there was much consternation. They realized, as I did, that this was an extremely formidable force, and chances for a successful attack and return was extremely doubtful. I advised their flight leader that I would be making an attack, and would like to co-operate with them. He said they were bombed up and were ready to go and had no desire to wait. They would continue to a different airfield on completion of their attack.

'I returned to my airplan. The crew had the bombs off the truck and ready for loading, but we had no bomb hoist available. This created a great problem as there was no means that I could see to load these bombs other than by hoisting them up in the bomb bay manually.

Three of my crewmen started rolling the bombs underneath the bomb bay. Three were all that could get around the bomb-bay and stand in the particular section where the bombs were to be loaded. The forward portion of the bomb-bay was loaded with fuel tanks. The two aft sections were where we were to load these bombs. These three men then performed a feat that I would believe to be impossible had I not witnessed it. These men were LTJG Garner Culpepper, Aviation Ordnanceman Lee Little and my Bombardier Lee Weber.

'After rolling the bombs under the bomb-bay, Little and Weber got on each end of the bomb and heaved it up about two feet. Culpepper then slid under on his hands and knees to hold the bomb while Little and Weber got a new hold on it. Then all three gave a mighty heave and latched the bomb on to the bomb shackle. This was done in darkness in the small section of the bomb-bay, and I truly believe this to be an act that is almost unequalled. Thinking back on it, while all three of these men were fairly large and well muscled, I cannot understand how Culpepper was able to hold those bombs on his back while on his hands and knees even for a short period of time. In addition, latching the bomb lugs into the shackle required a good deal of juggling even when using a bomb hoist. Getting these four bombs into the airplane continues to amaze me.

'Once the bombs were loaded, it was dark and I turned and called the rest of the crew to get up from slit trenches and come over to the airplane. I told them that we were going to make an attack against this force and it was time to go. They all realized the implications but no one objected and they all manned the aircraft. After the engines were started I taxied down the strip and lined up with what I hoped was the runway ahead. There were no lights or flare pots to light the runway. I put on full power and the aircraft started rolling very slowly. At first the left wheel sank into the dirt and I swerved left. I applied heavy right brake only to have the right wheel sink into the dirt and I swerved right as a result. Several more swerves occurred but we were gradually accelerating. Soon I could see some trees and under-brush looming out of the darkness and realized that it was now or never. I pulled hard on the elevator control and the airplane literally staggered into the air. After raising the gear-flaps, I began climbing, paralleling the west coast of Mindoro. Approximately fifty miles north, I reached 8,000 feet and could see and hear on the radio a great deal of action going on. As I approached the force I could see the Army B-25s starting their attacks. A big bright moon had just come up in the east and the area was fairly well illuminated. I could see the B-25s starting their attacks at low level, strafing as they went in. The return fire from the Japanese ships was extremely heavy and I saw several of the B-25s burst into flames and crash.

One flaming B-25 crashed into the Japanese destroyer. It appeared to me that the B-25s were taking a terrific beating, and not many were getting through with their attacks. I decided to swing on round to the west and launch my attack into the moon to better my chances of approaching undetected.

'I turned towards the force from the west, directed by my radarman, Allen B. Anania. As he called eight miles from the task force, my bombardier came up and said "I have them visually, follow PDI." The PDI being the needle on the pilot's instrument panel that signalled the direction of the turn for the bombing run. I was evidently undetected as the Japanese force continued firing at the low level B-25s attacking from the other direction. I told Weber, my bombardier, to pick out the largest ship and to make sure of a hit. If he did not like the set-up on this bombing run, we would break it off and try again. Closing in further we opened bomb bay doors and I asked Weber to ensure that the bombs were armed and ready. Shortly thereafter Weber called "Bombs away" and I immediately made a hard right turn. At this point the Japanese evidently had detected us and heavy AA fire was directed upwards towards us. As I looked back down after rolling out of my right turn, I, along with Weber and several others in the crew, observed one burst in the wake of the ship and two or three identifiable bomb bursts on the heavy cruiser. There was a feeling of great pleasure and satisfaction at this point. The Japanese ships continued to fire wildly and steaming at extremely high speeds. We retired a short distance from the vessels and reported our hits upon the heavy cruiser.

'Prior to this time, we had sent a contact report on initially regaining contact with the force. At this time I reported by radio that one destroyer was sunk by Army B-25s and the heavy cruiser had been damaged and was streaming oil. My bombardier was overjoyed with having hit a major unit of the Japanese fleet. He repeatedly said over the airplane's interphone "Let's go get more bombs. Let's go get more bombs." This, of course, was out of the question, for if we returned to Leyte we would not have had time to attack again that night. Landing at Mindoro was out of the question as the task force was approaching and would soon heavily shell the area.

'At this point I broke off tracking and started my flight towards home base at Tacloban. Both myself and my crew were completely exhausted having been airborne for about twenty-four hours.

The foregoing account typifies the atmosphere and over-all hazards of US Navy Liberator operations in the Pacific during those days. The authorities recognized this and Paul Stevens was awarded the Navy Cross and all the crew received the Distinguished Flying Cross.

Pacific Privateers

Complaints about the B-24s handling characteristics were many and suggestions filtered through from all theatres of war on how to improve the Liberator's performance. The US Navy in particular required more armament and armour for their 'mast-head' bombing runs on Japanese shipping while B-24 airmen in all war zones requested better stability. At the same time Consolidated engineers recognized the need for a new patrol aircraft capable of accommodating the considerable advances in radio navigational aids and RCM apparatus.

In April 1943 Consolidated and the US Navy got together and decided that the PB2Y-3 Coronado flying boat programme should end and production of a new patrol bomber based on the B-24's high aspect ratio wing and tricycle undercarriage should begin. The Liberator's fuselage was stretched by seven feet to 74 feet 7 inches to make room for the new electronics and more powerful Twin Wasps were installed. A new single fin replaced the twin-tailed empennage of the B-24 and this improved stability. The introduction of a

dorsal turret complemented the mid-upper turret while a second 0.50 calibre machine gun was installed in each of the waist positions. All this additional weight was offset to some extent by the removal of the ball turret.

The US Navy liked the new breed of Liberator which was designated PB4Y-2, and in October 1944 placed an order for 710. Initially, three PB4Y-1 (B-24D) Liberators were modified to the new configuration but tests to improve lateral and directional stability revealed the need for a taller vertical fin. The newly designed patrol bomber was named the 'Privateer' by the Navy while USAAF versions simply became the B-24N. The first 'Privateer' mission of the war was flown by VPB118 on 14 January 1945.

By the end of the war, seven of the US Navy's Liberator squadrons in the Pacific had been equipped with the 'Privateer' at one time or another. The PB4Y-2s ranged throughout the Pacific from Singapore in the south to Korea in the north, flying the longest overwater patrols of the war. They also flew Fleet Barrier Patrols

ahead of US Navy shipping, spotting and destroying the enemy before American seaborne movements could be reported. In March 1945 the Japanese early warning picket boats in the path of the Fifth Fleet were hounded and sunk by the 'Privateer' squadrons and in July 1945 the US Third Fleet cruised unhindered off the Japanese coastline under their protection.

The 'Privateer' was so successful that an RY-3 transport version was developed. Nineteen were allocated to the US Navy, four of which were used as VIP transports for the then Commandant General A. A. Vandergrift and his staff. The RAF also received twenty-seven RY-3s and the British Prime Minister, Winston Churchill, changed his LB-30 for one in 1944.

By the time the Pacific war was over, the 'Privateer' had proved to be as adaptable and accommodating as its forebear, the B-24 Liberator, incorporating its strengths and benefitting from its weaknesses.

Photo Credits